The Siege of Derry in Ulster Protestant Mythology

THE
SIEGE OF DERRY
IN ULSTER PROTESTANT
MYTHOLOGY

Ian McBride

FOUR COURTS PRESS • DUBLIN

Set in 12 on 15 point Bembo for
FOUR COURTS PRESS • DUBLIN
55 Prussia St, Dublin 7, Ireland
e-mail: fcp@ indigo.ie
and in North America for
FOUR COURTS PRESS LTD
c/o ISBS, 5804 N.E. Hassalo Street, Portland, OR 97213.

© Ian McBride 1997

A catalogue record for this title
is available from the British Library.

ISBN 1-85182-299-2

Printed in Ireland
by ColurBooks Ltd, Dublin

Contents

Preface

This project was completed while I was a research fellow at Corpus Christi College, Cambridge, and I am delighted to have the opportunity to express my gratitude to the Master and Fellows of Corpus for their generosity and support. Toby Barnard, Marianne Elliott, Roy Foster and Alvin Jackson have all helped me by reading and commenting on the manuscript. I owe them thanks for their valuable suggestions and criticisms, and apologies for not being able to follow up all of them. For advice on various points I am indebted to Tony Crowe, chairman of the Walker Trust, and to James Kelly. The librarians and archivists at the Union Theological College, the Linenhall Library and the Public Record Office of Northern Ireland also deserve thanks. Finally, the enthusiasm and efficiency of Ronan Gallagher at Four Courts Press has been greatly appreciated.

Ian McBride
University of Durham

The Siege of Derry in
Ulster Protestant Mythology[1]

At the centre of Ulster Protestant culture lies a cycle of myths concerning the seventeenth-century struggle between Protestant and Catholic, settler and native, for supremacy in Ireland.[2] The highpoint of the Protestant calendar is the Twelfth of July, the anniversary of the Battle of the Boyne (1690), still kept as a bank holiday in Northern Ireland. By comparison, the parades held to commemorate the shutting of the gates of Derry (18 December

1   Problems of nomenclature arise in any discussion of Northern Ireland, but particularly in this case. When a British colony was established at Derry as part of the plantation of Ulster, the city was rechristened 'Londonderry' in honour of the London merchant companies who had funded the project. Today the name of the city functions as a shibboleth: Loyalists value the prefix as a reminder of the British connection, while Nationalists object to it for the same reason. In 1984 the Nationalist-controlled council voted to change its name to Derry City Council, but the official title of the city itself remains unaltered. Here I have followed a convention sometimes used by historians, referring to the city as 'Derry' and reserving the full title for the county.

2   For the place of seventeenth-century events in the Protestant imagination, see J.G. Simms, 'Remembering 1690', *Studies*, LXIII (1974), pp. 231-242; J.R. Hill, 'National Festivals, the State and 'Protestant Ascendancy' in Ireland, 1790-1829', *Irish Historical Studies*, XXIV (1984-5), pp. 30-51; idem, 'Popery and Protestantism, Civil and Religious Liberty: The Disputed Lessons of Irish History, 1680-1812', *Past and Present*, no. 118 (1988), pp. 96-129; Toby Barnard, 'The Uses of the 23 October 1641 and Irish Protestant Celebrations', *EHR*, CVI (1991), pp. 889-920; idem, '1641: A Bibliographical Essay', in B. MacCuarta (ed.), *Ulster 1641: Aspects of the Irish Rising* (Belfast, 1993), pp. 173-86; Brian Walker, '1641, 1689,

1688) and the relief of the city (12 August 1689) are local affairs.[3] It is the Siege of Derry, however, which is the key episode for loyalists. Oliver MacDonagh has described it as 'their original and most powerful myth', the classic embodiment of a bleak vision of the past as 'an endless repetition of repelled assaults, without hope of absolute finality or of fundamental change'.[4] For A.T.Q. Stewart, the Derry crisis establishes a paradigm for the entire history of Ulster Protestantism since the plantation; it is scarcely surprising, then, that he should have entitled his own protest against the Anglo-Irish Agreement 'The Siege of Ulster'.[5] The events of 1689 continue to echo in the titles of recent books such as Arthur Aughey's *Under Siege: Ulster Unionism and the Anglo-Irish Agreement* (1989), and Brian Follis's *A State under Siege: The Establishment of Northern Ireland, 1920-1925* (1995).

The Siege of Derry carries an emotional charge that the more famous Battle of the Boyne lacks. In part, this is simply because the 'Maiden City', unlike the River Boyne, is situated within the

1690 and All That: The Unionist Sense of History', *Irish Review*, no. 12 (Spring/Summer 1992), pp. 56-64; James Kelly, ' "The Glorious and Immortal Memory": Commemoration and Protestant Identity in Ireland 1660-1800', *Proceedings of the Royal Irish Academy*, vol. 94C (1990), pp. 25-52. The early decades of the twentieth century have supplied additional dates for the loyalist calendar: see Alvin Jackson, 'Unionist Myths 1912-1985', *Past and Present*, no. 136 (1992), pp. 164-85; idem, 'Unionist History', in Ciaran Brady (ed.), *Interpreting Irish History: The Debate on Historical Revisionism 1938-1994* (Dublin, 1994), pp. 253-68; Edna Longley, 'The Rising, the Somme and Irish Memory', in idem, *The Living Stream: Literature and Revisionism in Ireland* (Newcastle, 1994), pp. 69-85.

3 The original dates, according to the Old Style Julian calendar used before 1752, were 7 December and 1 August. At the end of the eighteenth century the commemorations were moved to the 'New Style' dates, eleven days later.

4 Oliver MacDonagh, *States of Mind: A Study of Anglo-Irish Conflict 1780-1980* (London, 1983), p. 14.

5 A.T.Q. Stewart, *The Narrow Ground: Aspects of Ulster, 1609-1969* (London, 1977), p. 52; idem, 'The Siege of Ulster', *The Spectator*, 11 Jan. 1986, pp. 15-16.

six Ulster counties which became Northern Ireland in 1922; Ulstermen and women participated in the defence of Derry, and their descendants still live there. More importantly, however, the siege presents in dramatic form a series of lessons regarding the relationship between Ulster Protestants and their traditional enemies. Like other political myths, the story of the siege is invoked to legitimate present actions and attitudes, and while the narrative has retained its basic structure, each generation has found fresh meanings, emphasising or suppressing different components according to its own ideological needs.[6]

The events of 1688-89 have been commemorated in a rich variety of forms. The best known are the annual band parades and religious services organised by the Apprentice Boys organisation to mark the two anniversaries. Other traditional modes of remembrance include bell-ringing, bonfires, dining, drinking and dancing. Images from the siege have been depicted on stained glass windows in St Columb's Cathedral, the Guildhall and the Apprentice Boys' Memorial Hall, and in a number of paintings; the same scenes have been reproduced on Orange banners and

6   In speaking of the siege as a myth I do not intend to question its status in Irish historiography, as some Jacobite and revisionist scholars have sought to do. By political myths I mean stories about the past told to justify or undermine political institutions and practices; their usefulness depends not on their fidelity to the historical record, but their relevance to the contemporary situation. For historical works dealing with political myths, see Christopher Hill, 'The Norman Yoke', in idem, *Puritanism and Revolution: Studies in the Interpretation of the English Revolution of the Seventeenth Century* (London, 1958), pp. 50-122; E.J. Hobsbawm and T. Ranger (eds.), *The Invention of Tradition* (Cambridge, 1983); T. Curtis (ed.), *Wales: The Invented Nation: Essays on Culture and National Identity* (Bridgend, 1986); Raphael Samuel (ed.), *Patriotism: The Making and Unmaking of British National Identity* (London, 1989); M.G.H. Pittock, *The Invention of Scotland: The Stuart Myth and the Scottish Identity, 1638 to the Present* (London, 1991); Roy Porter (ed.), *Myths of the English* (Cambridge, 1993). Some of this literature is marred by a one-sided reading of popular myths and traditions as strategies devised by ruling elites to bolster traditional power structures in an age of mass politics.

murals.[7] Since 1689 the Protestant victory has also been celebrated in literature and in music. To popular songs such as 'Derry's
Walls' can be added prodigious quantities of verse, at least one
play, and a symphony commissioned by Derry City Council in
1989. Contemporary accounts of the siege have been reprinted
regularly, and the Londonderry Corporation sponsored Cecil
Davis Milligan's exhaustive *History of the Siege of Londonderry* to
mark the Festival of Britain in 1951. Dozens of memorials have
been erected in the old city, relics from the siege have been carefully preserved in the museum of St Columb's Cathedral, and the
walls themselves still stand intact. 'In truth', as Macaulay wrote,
'the whole city is to this day a monument of the great deliverance.'[8]

The basic themes of the siege myth—defiance, solidarity, sacrifice, deliverance—are obvious enough. The story serves to reinforce the social cohesion and political resolve of Ulster
Protestants by recalling the unchanging threat to their faith and
liberties posed by the Catholic majority in Ireland; 'No
Surrender', the watchword of the defenders of Derry, has become
the arch-slogan of loyalism. After 1689 the Relief of Derry was

7   The best known paintings are Folingsby's 'The Relief of Derry' in the
     Guildhall, Derry; 'The Relief of Derry' by William Sadler II (1782-1839),
     and 'The Relief of Derry' (1861) by James Magill, both in the Ulster
     Museum; others can be found in St Columb's Cathedral and the
     Guildhall. 'The Siege of Derry', one of two tapestries commissioned for
     the chamber of the Irish House of Lords and hung there in 1733, can still
     be seen in the Bank of Ireland (formerly Parliament House), Dublin. Bill
     Rolston's *Politics and Painting: Murals and Conflict in Northern Ireland*
     (London, 1991) includes a reproduction of Bobby Jackson's mural in the
     Fountain estate in Derry; dating from the 1920s, it is the oldest extant wall
     mural in Northern Ireland. For toasting glasses see Catriona MacLeod,
     'Some Drinking Glasses and a Medal by William Mossop Commemor-
     ative of the Siege of Derry, 1689', *Irish Sword*, XIII (1977-79), pp. 152-6.
8   Thomas Babington Macaulay, *The History of England from the Accession of
     James II* (5 vols., London, 1849-61), II, p. 239.

quickly assimilated to a providential reading of history which centred on the confrontation between the reformed religion and Rome. In the decades after 1845, when it became customary to mark the two anniversaries with religious services in the cathedral and in the First Presbyterian Church, sermons were preached demonstrating the hand of God's providence in history, and the liberation of the city was sometimes compared to the deliverance of the children of Israel from Egyptian bondage.[9] It is the other Derry anniversary, however, which grants the most revealing insights into loyalist mentality. Each year, on 18 December, the internal differences within the Protestant community are symbolically resolved as the Apprentice Boys Clubs re-enact the shutting of the gates. The climax of the day is the burning in effigy of the traitor Robert Lundy in what A.T.Q. Stewart has described as 'an act of ritual purgation'.[10] It is this schizophrenic memory of the siege—the fear of betrayal combined with the triumph of liberation—which guarantees its unique position in the loyalist mind.

This book examines the ways in which the siege has been remembered, commemorated, and interpreted over the last three centuries. It reviews the work of historians, pamphleteers and politicians who have sought to use the siege to reinforce later ideological positions. The relationship between the sectarian construction of 1689 and the whiggish interpretation, which placed the siege in the wider context of the constitutional struggle

---

9   See Thomas B. Gough, *A Sermon, Preached in the Cathedral of Derry, on Monday, December 18, 1826* (Derry, 1827); William McClure, *Sermon, Preached to the Apprentice Boys of Derry, on the Twelfth of August, 1859, Being the 170th Anniversary of the Relief of the City* [Derry, 1859]; Alexander Buchanan, *Sermon Delivered before the Orangemen of the City of Derry and the Cumber Claudy District on the Twelfth of July, 1849, at Brackfield Presbyterian Church* (Derry, 1849); Hugh Hanna, '*A Memorial of the Divine Mercies to our Fathers*', *Being a Sermon Delivered to the Apprentice Boys, in the Strand Presbyterian Church, on 12th August, 1863, the 174th Anniversary of Derry's Deliverance* (Derry, 1863).

10 Stewart, *Narrow Ground*, p. 67.

against the Stuart monarchy, is explored. At a different level, the anniversary parades held in Derry are used as a barometer of denominational and social antagonisms. Although Belfast has always been the capital of Ulster Unionism, it is Northern Ireland's second city, precariously situated on the edge of the Ulster plantation, which has been the most sensitive register of Protestant apprehensions. It was Derry which felt most keenly the demographic pressures of Catholic migration in the first half of the nineteenth century; after 1885 the marginal constituency of Derry City became the key seat in a province divided evenly between Catholic Nationalism and Protestant Conservatism; under the Stormont regime Derry became the *locus classicus* of Unionist corruption and the crucible of the Civil Rights movement; finally, it was the Relief celebrations of August 1969 which ignited Catholic resentment and led to the deployment of British troops on the streets of Northern Ireland.

The historical vision described below is more complex than the conventional picture of fear and loathing. A survey of the ways in which the siege has been remembered does not support the received image of a homogeneous people united against the common enemy; on the contrary, it reveals a community deeply divided along lines of ideology, religious denomination and class. In the first period examined—the decades between the 1690s and the 1730s—the story of the siege became a central issue in the power-struggle between Anglicans and Presbyterians in the northern province. In the later half of the eighteenth century a new, Patriot, interpretation arose, which stressed the constitutional benefits of the Glorious Revolution and played down the sectarian dimension with the result that not only Dissenters but also Catholics felt able to join in the annual festivities held in the city. This fragile ecumenism could not withstand the reassertion of sectarian identities in the 1790s, however, and the double threat of republican insurrection and French invasion forced a retreat to seventeenth-century attitudes, a process continued during O'Connell's agitation for Catholic emancipation in the 1820s. As

[14]

the Catholic population of Derry began to expand, the annual parades provoked a series of sectarian confrontations, although a whiggish interpretation of the siege survived among the spokesmen of Ulster Liberalism. The final section considers the use of siege symbolism in Unionist rhetoric from the Home Rule crises of 1886-1922 to the period of disillusionment and disinheritance inaugurated in 1969. Before turning to this survey, however, it may be helpful to sketch a brief outline of the events which form the basis of the siege myth.

I

The story of the Siege of Derry—'the most memorable in the annals of the British isles'[11]—began on 7 December 1688 when thirteen apprentices barred the city gates against the earl of Antrim's Catholic army. The regiment of Lord Mountjoy, composed largely of Protestants, had been summoned to Dublin, leaving the city without a garrison. James II, still rightful king, now controlled most of Ireland, but the walled city of Derry was of vital importance to his struggle to recover the throne of the three kingdoms from William of Orange. At this critical moment, the actions of the Protestant inhabitants, which would inspire so many future generations of loyalists, were shaped by their own inherited memories of the struggle between Planter and Gael. Captain Thomas Ash recorded in his diary fearful reports that the Roman Catholics intended to rise 'and to act over the tragedy of

---

11 Macaulay, *History of England*, III, p. 237. The best accounts of the siege are Cecil Davis Milligan, *History of the Siege of Londonderry 1689* (Belfast, 1951); Tony Gray, *No Surrender! The Siege of Londonderry 1689* (London, 1975); Patrick Macrory, *The Siege of Derry* (Oxford, 1988). For the wider context see J.G. Simms, *Jacobite Ireland, 1685-91* (London, 1969); Robert Beddard (ed.), *The Revolutions of 1688* (Oxford, 1981); Jonathan I. Israel (ed.), *The Anglo-Dutch Moment: Essays on the Glorious Revolution and its World Impact* (Cambridge, 1991).

one thousand six hundred and forty-one', rumours which were apparently confirmed by the discovery and circulation of the famous 'Comber letter'.[12] As in 1641, Protestant settlers from the surrounding countryside were fleeing to the city for refuge.

As fears of a Catholic rising mounted, civic leaders in Derry, aware of the poor state of the city's fortifications and reluctant to defy the authority of their legitimate king, found themselves unable to decide on a course of action. 'While we were in this confused hesitation', recalled Ash, 'a few resolute APPRENTICE BOYS determined for us: these ran to the gates and shut them, drew up the bridge, and seized the magazine. This, like magic, roused an unanimous spirit of defence, and now with one voice we determined to maintain the city at all hazards, and each sex and age joined in the important cause.'[13] The first component in the story of the siege, then, is the call for popular mobilisation and resolute action. The shutting of the gates was an overt act of rebellion against royal authority, setting a vital precedent for the replacement of pusillanimous leaders with new hardliners. In contemporary accounts the apprentices were referred to as 'the mob', 'the mobile', 'the rabble' or the 'younger' and 'meaner' sort:[14] in the siege myth it is always the ordinary, lower class Protestants who supply their own means of salvation.

The second scene revolves around the threat posed by doubters, appeasers and traitors. Resistance to King James was condemned by Ezekial Hopkins, the Episcopalian bishop of Derry, who explained that the closing of the gates was a sinful act

12 John Hempton, *The Siege and History of Londonderry* (Derry, Dublin and London, 1861), p. 280.
13 Quoted in Milligan, *Siege of Londonderry*, pp. 34–5. The thirteen original apprentices were Henry Campsie, William Crookshanks, Robert Sherrard, Daniel Sherrard, Alexander Irwin, James Steward, Robert Morrison, Alexander Cunningham, Samuel Hunt, James Spike, John Cunningham, William Cairns and Samuel Harvey.
14 For examples see ibid., pp. 37, 40; George Walker, *A True Account of the Siege of London-Derry* (London, 1689), p. 12. At the end of the seventeenth century the terms 'apprentices' and 'mob' could be used interchangeably.

of disobedience. But the real villain of the siege drama is Lieutenant-Colonel Robert Lundy, a Scottish Episcopalian who had been appointed military governor of the city. Although Macaulay concluded that his conduct should be attributed to 'faint-heartedness and to poverty of spirit' rather than Jacobitism,[15] it is clear that Lundy was incompetent as a military leader, that he had decided that Derry was indefensible, and that he eventually advised that the city should come to terms with the Jacobites. In the face of popular opposition, led by the young Ulster-Scot Adam Murray, Lundy resigned his authority and Major Henry Baker and the Rev. George Walker[16] were appointed as the military and civil governors of the besieged city. The disgraced leader was allowed to escape from Derry disguised as a private soldier.

The expulsion of Lundy is usually seen as the point of no return in Derry's abjuration of James II, but it was only in April 1689, when William and Mary were crowned in England, that the citizens declared unambiguously for the new king. The primary sources reveal that the garrison continued to be plagued by doubts and divisions. In early May a quarrel between Henry Baker and Colonel John Mitchelburne led to a scuffle in which Mitchelburne was wounded and then placed under house arrest. A Council of Fourteen was then set up to act as a check on the two governors following signs of discontent in the garrison. The

---

15 Macaulay, *History of England*, III, p. 188.
16 George Walker (c. 1645-90), embodiment of the church militant; matriculated Trinity College Dublin, 1662; rector of Donoughmore, County Tyrone, 1674; raised a regiment at Dungannon, 1688; joint governor of Derry during the siege, first with Henry Baker, then John Mitchelburne; killed at the Boyne, 1690. Bones said to be Walker's were recovered from the Boyne and buried in the church at Castle Caulfield, Co. Tyrone by his widow. A phrenological examination made of the skull in 1854 concluded that Walker's was 'rather a clear and controlling, than a profound or comprehensive intellect'. See Abraham Dawson, 'Biographical Notice of George Walker, Governor of Derry during the Siege in 1688 [sic]', *Ulster Journal of Archaeology*, 1st ser., II (1854), p. 278.

fear of traitors within the gates continued to distract the defenders throughout the siege: even Walker, who was believed to have a private hoard of food hidden in his house, was suspected of disloyalty. On one occasion, when a mob ransacked his quarters and unearthed his private stock of beer, he was forced to flee to Baker's quarters for safety. There was also a steady flow of desertions from the city and a number of citizens were later reported to be in daily correspondence with the enemy. In popular versions of the tale, however, such awkward facts are not allowed to trip up the narrative. Thus it is possible to find, in a recent study of loyalist mentality, that the siege began when 'in the face of indecision by the city governor, Lundy, Apprentice Boys shut the gates against the advancing James'.[17] In fact Lundy was not in Derry when the gates were closed; James II was not in Ireland at all.

It was not until April 1689, after negotiations with the Jacobites had finally broken down, that the investment of the city began in earnest. Over the next fifteen weeks the defenders of Derry—their number is usually put at 30,000—fought against the combined forces of Jacobite bombardment, disease and famine. After an unsuccessful assault on the walls led by the earl of Clancarty at the end of June, the Jacobites concentrated on a blockade in an attempt to starve the garrison into submission, and it was hunger and illness, rather than military action, which accounted for most of the 10,000 deaths reported at the end of the ordeal. Perhaps the most haunting image of the siege is that of the starving citizens reduced to a diet of horse flesh, dogs, cats, rats and mice, tallow and starch. On 13 June a relief expedition led by Major-General Percy Kirke reached the River Foyle, but it was not until over six weeks later that the merchant ship *The Mountjoy*, captained by the ill-fated Micaiah Browning, broke

17 Anthony Buckley, 'Uses of History among Ulster Protestants', in Gerald Dawe and John Wilson Foster (eds.), *The Poet's Place: Ulster Literature and Society: Essays in Honour of John Hewitt, 1907-87* (Belfast, 1991), p. 262.

through the boom which the Jacobites had erected across the river.[18] On the night of 31 July, after one hundred and five days, the enemy decamped: the siege was over.

The final element in the story concerns the behaviour of the English after the liberation of the city. Under Kirke's despotic rule, the garrison's eight regiments were halved to four and new captains were appointed from among Kirke's friends; rates of pay were reduced, and Kirke failed to protect the houses and farms of the Protestants in the surrounding countryside from Jacobite marauders. After Kirke's departure the honeymoon period with the relieving army came to an end as friction between the English troops and the local inhabitants developed. But there was worse still to come. Despite a flow of petitions and memorials to parliament over the next twenty-five years, the officers and men of the garrison were never paid.[19] It was calculated that they were owed £195, 091 in wages and another £138,349 for the purchase of arms and for property damaged by the enemy.[20] Although the House of Commons looked into the matter on several occasions, nothing was done. William Hamill, acting as agent for the garrison, battled for thirty years; eventually he was imprisoned for debt, and published from his London gaol a bitter account of his ordeal entitled *A View of the Danger and Folly of Being Publick-Spirited, and Sincerely Loving One's Country* (1721). The brave defenders, meanwhile, were left 'to drop into their Graves, one after another, through Hunger, Cold and other Extremities of Misery; and many of them could not have found

---

18 Macaulay described how Browning 'died by the most enviable of all deaths', shot in the head during the liberation of his native city: *History of England*, III, p. 236. His death scene, as Owen Dudley Edwards has pointed out to me, inspired Walt Whitman's 'Oh Captain, My Captain', written upon the assassination of Abraham Lincoln.

19 Many of these petitions can be found in the British Library in 'Tracts Relating to Scotland and Ireland' (816 m.17).

20 William Hamill, *A View of the Danger and Folly of Being Publick-Spirited, and Sincerely Loving One's Country* (London, 1721), p. 5.

Graves to lie down in, if it had not been for the conveniency of the Living; their Poverty being such, that few of them had enough to Fee the Parish-Officers, for a Christian Burial.'[21] After Hamill's failure they gave up: the British debt to the defenders of Derry was never settled.

II

The defeat of the Jacobite forces in the war of 1689-91 laid the foundations of a Protestant Ascendancy in Ireland which was to endure for over a hundred years. Even at its most confident, however, the Protestant elite bore the scars of seventeenth-century battles, reinforcing a siege mentality which found expression in the penal code. Sir John Temple's *The Irish Rebellion* (1646), regularly reprinted throughout the eighteenth century, memorialised the atrocities committed during the rising of 1641, calling for a 'wall of separation' to be built between the colonists and the genocidal natives.[22] The need for eternal vigilance against popery was echoed by another popular work, William King's *The State of the Protestants in Ireland* (1691), which dwelt upon the wicked designs of the Catholics in the reign of James II to reverse the land settlement and destroy Protestantism. Throughout the eighteenth century the anniversaries of these two pivotal events were marked by commemorative sermons which hailed each miraculous deliverance of Protestant Ireland as a providential intervention on behalf of a divinely favoured people. As historians have long recognised, the idea of the Irish nation articulated by the Ascendancy in the century after the Boyne rested upon the exclusion of the defeated native population from public life. But it also demanded the suppression of those other Protestants who

---

21 Ibid., p. 5.
22 Thomas Bartlett, *The Fall and Rise of the Irish Nation: The Catholic Question 1690-1830* (Dublin, 1992), p. 9.

dissented from the established church, and in particular the mass of Ulster-Scots who cherished their own bitter memories of 1641 and 1689.

In the besieged city of Derry, Churchmen and Dissenters had submerged their religious and political differences in the face of the common threat. An arrangement was reached whereby members of the established church used the cathedral on Sunday mornings and their non-conformist allies held services there in the afternoon. 'The Londerias', a poem written by a Derry soldier named Joseph Aickin, celebrated this solidarity:

> The Church and Kirk do thither jointly go
> In opposition to the common foe:
> Although in time of peace they disagree,
> Yet they sympathize in adversity.[23]

In the second half of the nineteenth century loyalist orators would hark back to this moment of unity in their attempts to play down the disagreements which continued to trouble the Protestant community. If a closer look is taken at the coalition of 1689, however, cracks soon begin to emerge.

There can be little doubt, for example, that the Ulster Presbyterians had been noticeably less inhibited than their Episcopalian brethren in organising resistance to James II. They were quick to welcome William after his landing in England on 4 November—two commissioners, Patrick Adair of Belfast and John Abernethy of Moneymore, were sent to wait on the Prince of Orange *before* he was proclaimed king—and Presbyterian clergymen had been active in raising troops at an early stage. In Derry it seems to have been a Dissenting minister, the Rev. James Gordon of Glendermot, who first advised the barring of the city against the king's troops. The majority of the Apprentice Boys

---

23 Quoted in Thomas Witherow, *Derry and Enniskillen in the Year 1689: The Story of Some Famous Battlefields in Ulster* (Belfast, 1873), p. 258.

were also Presbyterians, as was David Cairns of Knockmany in County Tyrone, the first citizen of any standing to publicly identify himself with them.[24]

Such zeal for the Williamite cause was facilitated by the contractual understanding of political obligation espoused by Scottish Calvinists in the seventeenth century. Well versed in resistance theory, the Presbyterians demonstrated few scruples about the deposition of a tyrannical monarch. The Anglican church, on the other hand, had invested heavily in the divine right theory of kingship since the Restoration. After the city gates had been closed, Dr Ezekial Hopkins, the bishop of Derry, had counselled passive obedience to royal authority; according to one account he was subsequently driven out of the city by 'Church-rebel *Jack Presbyter*'.[25] William King, who later emerged as the chief apologist of the Williamite revolution, had initially denounced the shutting of the gates as act of 'rank rebellion'.[26] His *State of the Protestants of Ireland* suggests that the defiance of Derry, which had taken place before the 'abdication' of James II, was still a source of embarrassment for conservative Anglicans.

24 James Seaton Reid, *History of the Presbyterian Church in Ireland*, ed. William D. Killen (2nd edn., 3 vols., Belfast, 1867), II, pp. 354-7, 366; James Kirkpatrick, *An Historical Essay upon the Loyalty of Presbyterians* (n.pl., 1713), p. 395; Witherow, *Derry and Enniskillen*, p. 39. Presbyterians also played a prominent role at the siege of Enniskillen: see William McCarmick, *A Farther Impartial Account of the Actions of the Inniskilling-Men* (London, 1691), published as a corrective to Andrew Hamilton's *A True Relation of the Actions of the Inniskilling-Men* (London, 1690). McCarmick's pamphlet was reprinted by the Rev. W.T. Latimer in 1896.

25 *An Apology for the Failures Charg'd on the Reverend Mr George Walker's Printed Account of the Late Siege of Derry, in a Letter to the Undertaker of a More Accurate Narrative of that Siege* (n.pl., 1689), p. 14.

26 Reid, *Presbyterian Church in Ireland*, II, pp. 424-5. For Anglican attitudes to the Glorious Revolution, see J.I. McGuire, 'The Church of Ireland and the 'Glorious Revolution' of 1688', in Art Cosgrove and Donal McCartney (eds.), *Studies in Irish History Presented to R. Dudley Edwards* (Dublin, 1979), pp. 137-49; Raymond Gillespie, 'The Irish Protestants and James II, 1688-90', *IHS*, XXVIII (1992), pp. 124-33.

King was forced to resort to the curiously legalistic argument that the inhabitants of Derry were bound to refuse entry to the Jacobite army by their foundation charter, which proclaimed the city 'a Shelter and Refuge for Protestants against the Insurrections and Massacres of the Natives'.[27] These theological and ideological antagonisms, largely forgotten during the Jacobite campaign, resurfaced once the emergency had passed.

The decade after the Revolution provided a dramatic boost to Irish Presbyterianism, as a massive wave of Scottish immigrants poured into the northern province. Recent demographic research has emphasised the importance of the final decades of the seventeenth century in establishing the denominational pattern of modern Ulster.[28] The poll-tax returns for 1660 show that, half a century after the official plantation had begun, British settlers were still a minority in every Ulster county; this situation was transformed by bursts of Scottish immigration in the 1650s, the late 1670s and particularly the 1690s, when low rents in Ulster coincided with a series of bad harvests in Scotland.[29] While contemporary estimates of this last great migration, ranging from 50,000 to 80,000, are certainly too high, they do testify to the mounting apprehensions of an increasingly beleaguered Anglican church.[30]

The rapid growth of the Scottish settlements was reflected in church expansion. Of the 148 Presbyterian congregations in exis-

---

27 *The State of the Protestants of Ireland under the Late King James's Government; in which their Carriage towards him is Justified, and the Absolute Necessity of their Endeavouring to Be Freed from his Government, and of Submitting to their Present Majesties is Demonstrated* (London, 1691), p. 103.

28 Louis Cullen, 'Population Trends in Seventeenth-Century Ireland', *Economic and Social Review*, VI, (1975), pp. 149-165. See also W. Macafee, 'The Colonisation of the Maghera Region of South Derry during the Seventeenth and Eighteenth Centuries', *Ulster Folklife*, XXIII (1977), pp. 70-91.

29 Cullen, 'Population Trends', pp. 153-7.

30 Ibid., p. 157.

tence in 1720, over half had been established since the Restoration, with as many as 44 originating in the years between 1691 and 1715.[31] In 1690, the year that the Kirk was established in Scotland, the Synod of Ulster was constituted. The creation of a rival ecclesiastical structure posed a direct challenge to the established church, and the Presbyterian system of church government, now functioning openly and efficiently for the first time, became an obsession with Anglican magistrates. From the end of the century, the episcopal courts were once more clamping down on Presbyterian marriages, funerals and schools, and a vigorous campaign was mounting for the full implementation of the penal laws against Dissent. Although the High Church backlash, which reached a highpoint under the Tory administration of 1710-14, was restrained by the imperial government, the establishment secured a lasting victory with the test act of 1704, which made the taking of the Anglican sacrament an essential qualification for public office.

As the Anglo-Irish elite consolidated its control over national and local politics, then, Protestant Dissenters once more found themselves relegated to the position of second class citizens.[32] The sense of betrayal nurtured during the reigns of William and Anne was heightened when the first great exodus from Ulster to the American colonies occurred between 1717 and 1720. Although historians have related Dissenting emigration to economic patterns, it was perceived by contemporaries as a direct response to religious persecution. The Rev. James McGregor of Aghadowey, a veteran of 1689, led his congregation across the Atlantic in 1718 'to avoid oppression and cruel bondage'.[33] Along with the Rev. Matthew Clerk, another siege survivor, he helped to found the

---

31 Alan Gailey, 'The Scots Element in Northern Irish Popular Culture', *Ethnologia Europaea*, VIII (1975), pp. 5-8.

32 Ian McBride, 'Presbyterians in the Penal Era', in *Bullán: A Journal of Irish Studies*, I, no. 2 (Autumn, 1994), pp. 73-86.

33 Edward L. Parker, *The History of Londonderry, Comprising the Towns of Derry and Londonderry, N.H.* (Boston, 1851), p. 34.

township of Londonderry in New Hampshire.[34] Throughout the century Presbyterian clergymen complained that, although they had fought for the Protestant cause at Derry and Enniskillen, they found themselves debarred from the political nation. As late as the tithe controversy of the 1780s, one clergyman would recall the humiliation of his ancestors: 'They assisted in conquering the Roman Catholicks, and were reduced to the same servitude.'[35] Memories of the Siege of Derry, far from unifying the Protestant population, helped to crystallise a separate Presbyterian culture of grievance.

The demography of Derry city, which had been transformed during the Restoration period from a centre of English culture into an Ulster-Scots stronghold, made it a battleground for the religious and party-political conflicts which followed the Glorious Revolution. When Bishop William King arrived at St Columb's in 1691, he found the Maiden City under siege, but this time the threat came from presbytery rather than popery. Some idea of the balance of power between the denominations can be obtained from the letters of William Nicolson, bishop of Derry between 1718 and 1722, who found within his parish 'about 400 families of Conformists in the whole; as many Popish; and no fewer than 800 Non-Conformists'.[36] Partly as a result of their control of local trade, the Dissenters formed a powerful party in the corporation, and Bishop King became embroiled in municipal politics as he sought, unsuccessfully, to prevent the election of non-conformists to the post of mayor.[37] These dis-

---

34 Ralph Stuart Wallace, 'The Scotch-Irish of Provincial New Hampshire', Ph.D. thesis, University of New Hampshire, 1984, ch. 4.

35 Samuel Barber, *Remarks on a Pamphlet, Entitled The Present State of the Church of Ireland, by Richard, Lord Bishop of Cloyne* (Dublin, 1787), p. 36.

36 Nicolson to Archbishop Wake, 1 August 1718, British Library, Wake Correspondence, Add. MSS. 6117, p. 127 (originals in Christ Church College, Oxford).

37 J.C. Beckett, 'William King's Administration of the Diocese of Derry 1691-1703', *IHS*, IV (1944), pp. 174-5.

putes were brought to an end by the implementation of the test act in 1704; significantly, Derry was the first corporation where the new legislation was applied. A tablet in the vestibule of the First Presbyterian Church in Magazine Street records the names of the ten aldermen, six of them former mayors, and fourteen burgesses who were forced to resign.

Before his move to the north King had already acquired a reputation as a militant defender of establishment Anglicanism. Having failed to persuade the government to revive the penal laws against non-conformity, he now launched a propaganda drive among the local Presbyterian population.[38] We know that attacks on Dissent figured prominently in his own sermons,[39] and in 1694 he collected together his arguments against non-conformity in *A Discourse Concerning the Inventions of Men in the Worship of God*. A rejoinder was quickly issued by the local Presbyterian minister, the Rev. Robert Craghead, dedicated to 'the mayor, aldermen and burgesses of Derry, of the Presbyterian persuasion'.[40] Following another exchange of pamphlets the controversy was concluded, but ill-feeling continued. In 1714 the Rev. James Blair, who had recently replaced Craghead, delivered two staunchly whiggish sermons to mark the accession of George I, in which he called for reconciliation between Church and Dissent and urged that the loyalty of Presbyterians entitled them to full citizenship. The defence of Derry, he observed, was crucial to the success of the Glorious Revolution,

> And, I hope, I may say it without envy, many of you in this Congregation, with your Brethren from other parts, were Active and successful by the blessing of God in that

38 Ibid., p. 172.
39 Ibid., p. 177.
40 Reid, *Presbyterian Church in Ireland*, II, p. 429. Craghead had taken refuge in Derry before fleeing to Scotland during the war: Thomas Witherow (ed.), *Historical and Literary Memorials of Presbyterianism in Ireland* (2 vols., Belfast, 1879-80), I, p. 89.

defence, and tho' several worthy Gentlemen of the
Establish'd Church did great service then. It[']s certain the
far greater number of such as carry'd Arms in this City
were of your Communion.[41]

Within the city walls, theological controversy thus intersected
with a fierce struggle for dominance in local government to frac-
ture the Protestant community which had held out against the
army of King James. The siege itself had become a source of con-
tention rather than a symbol of solidarity. On the First of August
1718, a double holiday marking both the relief of Derry and the
Hanoverian Succession, Nicolson informed the archbishop of
Canterbury that Churchmen and non-conformists had joined
together in celebration for the first time: 'from the day that K.
James's forces were put to flight, to this present, the Heart-burn-
ings of parties prevail'd so far, that they never could be brought
to an agreement in any common solemnity.'[42]

The religious and ethnic rivalry that cut through Irish
Protestantism was exacerbated by George Walker's *True Account of
the Siege of London-Derry* (1689), the most famous narrative of the
Derry crisis.[43] Walker, who had sailed from Derry on 9 August
1689, was hailed as the hero of the siege throughout Scotland and

---

41 James Blair, *Divine Providence, the Security of the Crown and Subject: Two
Sermons Preach'd in London-Derry December 8. 1714. Being a Day of
Thanksgiving, Observ'd by the Presbyterians of Ulster for the Peaceable and
Happy Accession of his Most Excellent Majesty King George to the Throne of
these Kingdoms* (Belfast, 1715), p. 28.

42 Nicolson to Archbishop Wake, 1 August 1718, British Library, Wake
Correspondence, Add. MSS. 6117, p. 128.

43 The first history of the siege was *A True and Impartial Account of the Most
Material Passages in Ireland since December 1688. With a particular Relation of
the Forces of Londonderry: Being Taken from the Notes of a Gentleman who was
Eye-witness to Most of the Actions Mention'd Therein, during his Residing there*
(London, 1689), published anonymously by Captain Joseph Bennet and
licensed in July 1689. News of the Derry conflict had also been released
in the government sponsored *London Gazette*.

[27]

England. He was presented with the freedom of the cities of Glasgow and Edinburgh, and after a triumphal progress south he was mobbed in London. He collected doctorates from Oxford and Cambridge, £5,000 from the House of Commons and was promised the bishopric of Derry.[44] Walker's portrait was painted by the court artist Sir Geoffrey Kneller; a copper plate was then struck off by the celebrated Dutch engraver Pieter Van Der Banck and prints were distributed throughout the kingdom.[45] In London there was a huge appetite for news of the Derry garrison, and Walker's *True Account*, published on 13 September, ran through several editions in the course of a few weeks. Further editions followed in Dublin (1736), London (1758) and Derry (1787).[46]

Like King's *State of the Protestants*, Walker's pamphlet viewed the defeat of the Jacobites as a manifestation of divine providence. 'God has Espoused your Majesties Cause', he declared in his dedication, 'and Fights your Battels, and for the Protestant Religion'.[47] In a bloodthirsty sermon, originally preached on the relief of Derry, he set the siege against the background of earlier rebellions, drawing the conclusion that 'a *Papist* is a *Papist* still,

---

44 Witherow, *Derry and Enniskillen*, pp. 260-64.
45 MacLeod, 'Some Drinking Glasses and a Medal by William Mossop', p. 153.
46 George Walker, *The Power of Protestant Religious Principle in Producing a National Spirit of Defence, Exemplified in a Diary of the Siege of London-Derry ... Now Published as a Useful Lesson to the Present Times* (London, 1758); idem, *A True Account of the Siege of London-Derry ... To which is Added, Sir John Dalrymple's Account of the Siege of Derry, and the Battle of the Boyne* (Londonderry, 1787). Douglas mentions the 1736 edition in his *Derriana*, but I have been unable to find a copy. See also George Walker, *A Sermon being an Incouragement for Protestants, of Happy Prospect of Glorious Success: With Exhortations to be Valiant against our Enemies, in Opposing the Bloody Principles of Papists, and Errors of Popery, &c. Occasionally on the Protestants['] Victory over the French and Irish Papists before London-Derry, in Raising that Desperate Siege* (printed London, reprinted Edinburgh, 1689).
47 Walker, *True Account*, 'Epistle Dedicatory'.

where even the Principle of Religion instils a kind of Fierceness and Barbarity into their Nature'.[48] But like King again, Walker had little time for Dissenters; their part in the conflict was marginalised. Although he carefully listed the eighteen Anglican clergymen who had served in the garrison, he claimed that he was unable to learn the names of the seven non-conformist ministers. In a later pamphlet he rectified this omission, but managed to offend the Presbyterians still further by referring to the Rev. Mr Gilchrist of Kilrea as Mr W. Kil-Christ.[49] Moreover, although he conceded that the Presbyterian ministers had kept their people 'very obedient and quiet', he accused Alexander Osborn, a Dissenting minister from Dublin, of being a Jacobite spy, and he claimed that David Houston, a member of the extreme Presbyterian sect of Cameronians, had stirred up religious animosities in Derry by trying to impose the Solemn League and Covenant upon its population.[50]

This was a challenge which the Presbyterians could not ignore. A satirical reply quickly appeared, designed to defend the memory of 'that great Body of Northern *Scots*', while the distinguished Dublin minister Joseph Boyse sprang to Osborn's defence.[51] Following the advice of a group of Irish émigrés then

---

48 Walker, *Incouragement for Protestants*, p. 6.

49 George Walker, *A Vindication of the True Account of the Siege of Derry in Ireland* (London, 1689), p. 33.

50 Walker, *True Account*, pp. 21, 57. See also Walker, *Vindication of the True Account*; [Anon.] *Reflections on a Paper, Pretending to be an Apology for the Failures Charged on Mr Walker's Account of the Siege of London-Derry* (London, 1689).

51 *An Apology for the Failures Charg'd on the Reverend Mr George Walker's Printed Account*, p. 2; Joseph Boyse, *A Vindication of the Reverend Mr Alexander Osborn, in Reference to the Affairs of the North of Ireland: in which Some Mistakes Concerning Him (in the Printed Account of the Siege of Derry; the Observations on it, and Mr Walker's Vindication of it) are Rectified. And a Brief Relation of those Affairs is Given so far as Mr Osborn, and Other N.C. Ministers in the North, were Concerned in 'Em* (London, 1690). The charges against Osborn were reiterated in N.N., *Some Remarks on Mr Bois [sic] Book in*

in Scotland, it was decided at a meeting held in Belfast on 5 November 1689 to send a deputation to London in order to tell the Presbyterian side of the siege story.[52] Without waiting for formalities, the Rev. John MacKenzie, who had been chaplain in Walker's regiment, departed for England.[53] His *Narrative of the Siege of Londonderry*, the fullest reply to Walker, emphasised the role of the Presbyterian clergy and gentry in the resistance, claiming that the Presbyterians had outnumbered Episcopalians by as many as fifteen to one.[54] Houston, he pointed out, had been deposed by the Presbytery of Route in 1687 and was not even in Derry during the siege. In sharp contrast to Walker's smug and self-centred narrative, MacKenzie made Colonel Adam Murray the hero of the conflict and belittled Walker's position, claiming that his authority had been confined to the care of provisions. He raised suspicions that Walker had treated with the Jacobites and embezzled the stores.[55] As for Walker's military exploits, MacKenzie wrote in a second pamphlet that he was 'guilty of Shedding no other Blood to Stain his Coat with, but that of the grape'.[56]

Defence of Osborn. And upon Some Passages in Mr Williams['] Sermon on the 23d of October Last. Sent in a Letter to Satisfie his Friend, a Dissenter in the Country (London, 1689).

52 Witherow, *Derry and Enniskillen*, I, pp. 68-9.

53 John MacKenzie, born Co. Down, 1649; educated Edinburgh; ordained Derryloran (Cookstown), 1673; chaplain to a regiment during the siege; returned to London 1694 to bring the persecution of Irish Presbyterians in the episcopal courts to the attention of King William; died 1697.

54 John MacKenzie, *A Narrative of the Siege of Londonderry: Or the Late Memorable Transactions of that City. Faithfully Represented, to Rectifie the Mistakes, and Supply the Omissions of Mr Walker's Account* (London, 1690), p. v.

55 Ibid., pp. 32, 36-7.

56 John MacKenzie, *Dr Walker's Invisible Champion Foyl'd: or, an Appendix to the Late Narrative of the Siege of Derry: wherein All the Arguments Offered in a Late Pamphlet to Prove it a False Libel, are Examin'd and Refuted* (London, 1690), p. 8.

Over the following year an undignified war of words followed as rival historians contested Walker's version of events. The Anglican interpretation was backed up by an anonymous pamphleteer, probably Dr John Vesey, a native of Coleraine who had deserted non-conformity and had been raised to the archbishopric of Tuam in 1678.[57] Several more tracts appeared before Walker ended the controversy and completed his apotheosis by getting himself killed at the Battle of the Boyne. Presbyterians inevitably returned to the issue in the 1730s, when a campaign for the repeal of the test was launched. Their spokesman was John Abernethy, the erudite pastor of the Wood Street congregation in Dublin, who himself had lost several brothers and sisters in the siege.[58] Rehearsing the services and sufferings of the Presbyterians at Londonderry, he contended that the ratio of Dissenters to Conformists within the walls had been at least ten to one.[59] The unity of Dissenters in the Williamite cause was once more contrasted with the Jacobite sympathies of High Churchmen after the bishop of Cloyne denounced Presbyterianism during the 1787 tithe controversy. The heroes of 1689 'had scarcely taught their children the story of their fame', lamented the Rev. William Campbell, when they 'beheld with indignation, that they were rendered by law incapable of serving that country, which they had just saved to the crown, and defended with such distinguished honour and gallantry'.[60]

---

57 [John Vesey?] *Mr John MacKenzyes [sic] Narrative of the Siege of London-Derry a False Libel: in Defence of Dr George Walker. Written by his Friend in his Absence* (London, 1690).

58 Reid, *History of the Presbyterian Church in Ireland*, III, p. 112, note 2.

59 John Abernethy, *Reasons for the Repeal of the Sacramental Test* (Dublin, 1733), p. 65, note.

60 William Campbell, *A Vindication of the Principles and Character of the Presbyterians of Ireland. Addressed to the Bishop of Cloyne, in Answer to his Book, Entitled The Present State of the Church of Ireland* (Belfast, 1788), p. 66. See also William Campbell to William Bruce, 29 September 1800, Public Record Office of Northern Ireland [hereafter PRONI], CR4/1/A3.

Presbyterian hatred of the egotistical Walker has proved remarkably persistent. Shortly after the appearance of Macaulay's *History of England* (1848-55), which tended towards the Anglican viewpoint, the Rev. William Killen republished MacKenzie's pamphlets in Belfast and Derry, reiterating the case against Walker.[61] The charges of cowardice, drunkenness and treachery were echoed by later ecclesiastical historians, such as Thomas Hamilton and William Latimer.[62] When the General Assembly met in Belfast in 1890, shortly before the bicentenary of the Battle of the Boyne, the Rev. H.B. Wilson complained that, although the rank and file of Derry defenders were Presbyterians, the only monument erected was to 'a worthless Episcopal rector'.[63] His remarks sparked off a controversy which began in the *Belfast Newsletter* and spread to *Newry Telegraph*, *Northern Whig* and *Tyrone Courier*. Although relations between the two churches have improved dramatically, the embers of this controversy were still glowing in the first half of this century.[64]

III

In the early eighteenth century, the Siege of Derry was not employed as a symbol of Protestant unity against the native Irish;

61 W.D. Killen (ed.), *MacKenzie's Memorials of the Siege of Derry Including his Narrative and Its Vindication* (Belfast and Derry, 1861), introduction.
62 Thomas Hamilton, *History of the Irish Presbyterian Church* (Edinburgh, 1886), p. 90; W.T. Latimer, *A History of the Irish Presbyterians* (Belfast, 1893), pp. 111-2.
63 *The Immortal Walker and the General Assembly. The Discussion between the Rev. Robert Oswald and the Rev. H.B. Wilson, D.D., Ex-Moderator of the General Assembly* (Newry, 1890), p. 6.
64 Rev. A.F. Moody, *Memories and Musings of a Moderator* (London, n.d.), pp. 93-108; Rev. W.S. Kerr, *Walker of Derry* (Londonderry, 1938). See also R.L. Marshall's sermon preached in 1942 to mark the 300th anniversary of the first Irish presbytery, quoted in Rev. John Dunlop, *A Precarious Belonging: Presbyterians and the Conflict in Ireland* (Belfast, 1995), p. 26.

on the contrary, its appearance in the polemical literature of the period highlighted the profound schism in the Irish Protestant world. With the repeal of the sacramental test in 1780, Dissenters were readmitted to political life, but as the tithe controversy of the 1780s demonstrates, memories of the persecution which followed the Revolution could easily be rekindled. From the 1760s, however, a 'Patriot' movement emerged which adapted the language of whig constitutionalism in order to claim greater independence for the Dublin parliament; both Churchmen and Dissenters could unite on this platform. This alliance was embodied in the Volunteer companies which sprang up throughout the northern province after 1778. The era of Irish legislative independence known as 'Grattan's Parliament' coincided with a revival of interest in the Gaelic past, but eighteenth-century patriotism was not based on the assertion of ethnic or cultural difference. Irish Protestants, like the American colonists before them, claimed an equal share of the rights and privileges guaranteed by the British constitution: the Williamite revolution remained central to their political identity.

Although patriotism and Protestantism were closely linked, the disappearance of the Jacobite threat and the spread of more liberal attitudes towards 'popery' created a climate where Catholic spokesmen could also appeal to the British constitution. The convergence of Protestant and Catholic aspirations was demonstrated in 1788-9, when the local Roman Catholic clergy joined the spectacular processions held in Derry to mark the centenary of the siege. Within a few years, however, this fragile ecumenism was disrupted by the polarisation of Irish politics and by the danger of insurrection and invasion. By 1796 the underground network of the United Irishmen was beginning to spread north-west to Londonderry, Tyrone and Donegal, while in south Ulster a bitter sectarian war was raging between the Defenders and the newly-formed Orange Order. In the face of a Catholic *revanche*, the patriotism which had developed during the penal era began to disintegrate, its final demise marked by the extinction of the Dublin parliament in 1800.

The earliest recorded celebrations of the siege should be viewed in the context of a whig political culture, constructed in England and exported to the subordinate kingdoms and colonies of the British empire. The great constitutional and religious struggles of the seventeenth century were firmly rooted in the English national consciousness. Royal birthdays, patriotic landmarks, naval and military victories all supplied festive occasions for the celebration of Britain's 'happy' constitution. Among those dates which received the official blessing of church and state were 4 November (the birthday of William III) and 5 November (the anniversary of both the Gunpowder Plot and William's landing at Torbay in 1688).[65] The whig establishment legitimated its position by reference to a conservative interpretation of 'Revolution principles', and these state-sponsored festivals were used to underline the existing political and social order. The 1688 revolution was open to rival interpretations, however, and whig iconography was repeatedly appropriated by opposition politicians.[66] The Williamite anniversaries were also assimilated into an older tradition of street theatre which fused together whiggery and anti-Catholicism; since the 1670s this riotous world of ritu-

65 David Cressy, *Bonfires and Bells: National Memory and the Protestant Calendar in Elizabethan and Stuart England* (London, 1989). These holy days were associated with the Whigs; more to the Tories' liking were 30 January (the martyrdom of Charles I), and 29 May (the restoration of the monarchy), occasions which were often used to attack Dissenters. Another, distinctively Irish, holy day fell on 23 October, the anniversary of the 1641 rebellion. The military victories of the Williamite war were also celebrated, at a popular level, by Boyne and Aughrim societies in Dublin.

66 Nicholas Rogers, *Whigs and Cities: Popular Politics in the Age of Walpole and Pitt* (Oxford, 1989), ch. 10; Kathleen Wilson, 'Inventing Revolution: 1688 and Eighteenth-Century Popular Politics', *Journal of British Studies*, 28 (1989), pp. 349-86; Colin Haydon, *Anti-Catholicism in Eighteenth-Century England, c. 1714-80* (Manchester, 1993), pp. 30, 33-7, 234.

al had centred on effigy-burnings, with the Pope and the Pretender as favourite targets.[67]

Little is known about the observance of the Derry anniversaries until the appearance of the town's first newspaper, the *Londonderry Journal*, in June 1772. In that year we are told that the 'ancient custom' of commemorating the relief of the city was revived by the mayor, Hugh Hill. Three years later, the Independent Mitchelburne Club was founded by 'those sons of liberty who formerly met and commemorated that blessed day'.[68] The history of the Derry anniversaries over the previous 80 years, and their relationship to the Apprentice Boys parades of the nineteenth century, remains vague. According to the official history of the Orange Order, the first Apprentice Boys Club was formed by Colonel Mitchelburne himself in 1714. In that year, it is claimed, the First of August was celebrated in what would become the traditional fashion: the crimson flag was hoisted on the cathedral steeple, a church service was held, the cannon were fired over the walls, and in the evening a dinner at Mr James Bradley's hotel was followed by a dance in the town hall.[69] Unfortunately this account relies on a single piece of evidence which cannot be corroborated.[70] Was this really an ancient custom, or an example of the 'invented tradition'?

We do know that the departure of the Jacobite army from Derry in 1689 occasioned a 'day of joy' in the city, involving the

---

67 David Cressy, 'The Fifth of November Remembered', in Porter (ed.), *Myths of the English*, pp. 75-9; William L. Sachse, 'The Mob and the Revolution of 1688', *Journal of British Studies*, IV (1964), pp. 23-40.

68 Hempton (ed.), *Siege and History of Londonderry*, pp. 415-8.

69 [R.M. Sibbett] *Orangeism in Ireland and throughout the Empire* (2 vols., London [1939]), pp. 190-1.

70 The information was supplied by Benjamin J. Darcus, Lieutenant-Governor of the Apprentice Boys, 1918-1921. Darcus belonged to an old Derry family; one ancestor had been witness to Mitchelburne's will. See Cecil Davis Milligan, *Colonel John Mitchelburne, Defender of Londonderry and the Mitchelburne Club of Apprentice Boys of Derry: Centenary of the Revival of the Club, 1854-1954* (Londonderry, 1954), p. 6.

beating of drums, the firing of cannon over the walls and the serving of free ale in the market place.[71] The diary of Captain Ash records that a week after the raising of the siege a service of thanksgiving was held in the St Columb's Cathedral and the city garrison fired three volleys and discharged the great guns three times.[72] The emergence of religious divisions in the 1690s, culminating in the implementation of the test act, seem to have marred the 'holy day' until 1718, when Bishop Nicolson officiated at divine service in the cathedral. Two years before, an elaborate celebration of the accession of George I had been organised by the city garrison, complete with effigies of the Pope, the Pretender, Ormond, Marr and Bolingbroke; but although one reference was made to the siege, most of the symbolism focused on the rival houses of Hanover and Stuart.[73] On the First of August 1718, as Nicolson recorded in his diary, the 'Bloody flag' was 'hoisted ye first time on ye steeple', the great guns were discharged and the day closed with a 'Splendid treat in ye Tolsel. Fireworks and illuminations'. He preached again in the cathedral two years later, and dined afterwards with Mitchelburne while bonfires burned in the town.[74] By the middle decades of the century the anniversary was marked by dinners organised by the Londonderry Corporation and by services in the cathedral.[75]

---

71 Walker, *Vindication*, p. 30.

72 Thomas Witherow (ed.), *Two Diaries of Derry in 1689* (Londonderry, 1888), pp. 102–3.

73 *An Account of the Procession at Londonderry, August 1st. 1716* (Dublin, n.d.), National Library of Ireland, LO folder 9/15.

74 Hempton (ed.), *Siege and History of Londonderry*, p. 411.

75 See, for example, minutes of the common council, 20 August 1753, PRONI, Corporation of Londonderry Minute Book 1742-53, LA 79/2A/6, p. 124; William Henry, *The Beauty, Deliverances, and Security of the British Constitution, set forth in a Sermon, Preached in the Cathedral Church of London-Derry, on the First Day of August, 1746* (Dublin, 1746). In 1748 twelve survivors of the siege attended an anniversary meeting at Magherafelt: *Universal Advertiser*, 16 Oct. 1759. I am grateful to James Kelly for this reference.

Some of the defenders themselves were clearly keen to ensure that their sufferings should not be forgotten. In 1689 Colonel Mitchelburne had placed the Jacobite colours captured at Windmill hill in the chancel of the cathedral, and he left in his will £50 for maintaining the crimson flag on the steeple; in 1713 he was permitted by Bishop Hartstronge to place a memorial inscription at the east window of the cathedral.[76] Mitchelburne was also reputed to be the author of the popular play *Ireland Preserv'd: or The Siege of Londonderry, Together with the Troubles of the North*, first published in Derry in 1705, reprinted in London (1708), Dublin (1738/9, 1777) Belfast (1744, 1750, 1759), Newry (1774), and Strabane (1787), and still popular in the hedge schools, among all denominations, in William Carleton's day.[77] It does not seem unlikely that Mitchelburne should have gathered around him other veterans of the siege each August, but no evidence of any formal 'Apprentice Boys' organisation has been found.[78]

We are on much firmer ground when we reach the revival of the celebration in 1772. On the morning of the First of August, according to the *Londonderry Journal*, bells were rung and the crimson flag was displayed on the steeple of the church. At noon the mayor, the corporation and the freemen assembled at the

---

76 Hempton (ed.), *Siege and History of Londonderry*, pp. 403, 410-11; Milligan, *Mitchelburne*, pp. 7-9.

77 J.R.R. Adams, *The Printed Word and the Common Man: Popular Culture in Ulster 1700-1900* (Belfast, 1987), p. 71.

78 Other such associations have been documented. The hard-drinking Dublin club, the Aldermen of Skinners' Alley, existed to commemorate the Protestants who had been purged from the Dublin corporation in 1687. Barrington believed it was the first Orange association ever formed: Hugh B. Staples (ed.), *The Ireland of Sir Jonah Barrington* (London, 1968), pp. 212-14. John Kearney's *A Sermon Preached at the Church of St. Warburgh's, Dublin, on Sunday the First Day of March, 1746-7. For the Benefit of the Poor Remains and Descendants of the Protestants who Defended Enniskilling and Derry in the Year 1689* (Dublin, 1747) mentions a charity set up for the veterans, widows and orphans of 1689 but tells us nothing further.

town hall and processed to the cathedral. Following a service there they returned to the town hall for dinner, and the day was concluded 'with illuminations, firings, and other tokens of joy'.[79] This custom continued throughout the 1770s, and we find a number of short-lived societies involved in the anniversary parades—the Phoenix Club (1773), the Independent Mitchelburne Club (1775), and the True Blue Society of the City and County of Londonderry (1776).[80] The Independent Mitchelburne Club was probably a whig dining society: in the last quarter of the century Ulster politics tended to divide between the 'independent interest', supported by the lesser gentry and the middle classes, and the aristocratic families who controlled most parliamentary seats.[81] After 1778, however, the ceremonies became dominated by the Volunteers corps.

The Volunteers were independent militia units, raised to defend Ireland against the French, but they quickly became a vehicle for the expression of Irish Protestant discontent with imperial government. Derry had raised three companies in 1778, among them the Apprentice Boys of Derry, the first organisation to go by that name, and it was natural that they should take over the local parades.[82] On 1 August 1778 the Volunteers marched to church for the first time; the following year they assembled afterwards to fire three volleys in the Diamond; and in 1779 we find them going through the ceremony of closing the gates on 7 December.[83] The frenetic marching and drilling of these years transformed public life throughout Protestant Ireland. Inevitably the glamour of volunteering recalled the military glories of past

79 Hempton (ed.), *Siege and History of Londonderry*, p. 415.

80 Ibid., pp. 417, 418, 420.

81 See Ian McBride, ' "Scripture Politics": The Religious Foundations of Presbyterian Radicalism in Late Eighteenth-Century Ireland', Ph.D. thesis, University of London, 1994, pp. 78-85. It is probably no coincidence that 1775 was an election year.

82 Hempton (ed.), *Siege and History of Londonderry*, p. 421.

83 Ibid., pp. 421-3. The 7th December was first marked in 1775: see ibid., p. 419.

days, and at a review held in Derry in 1780 the siege was re-enacted in mock array. So zealously did the these citizen-soldiers throw themselves into the performance that what began as a sham fight threatened to end in real bloodshed:

> the gallant lads attacked the walls with such material ardour that they burned the faces of their opponents, who were so much enraged, that it was with the utmost difficulty that they were restrained from returning real shot, and many now bear the honourable wounds of that glorious day.[84]

The upheavals of 1688-9 were by now firmly embedded in the local folk-memory. James Caldwell, a United Irishman born in 1769, recalled of his Derry schooldays that 'the cherished history of that chivalrous act of defence was almost a part of our scholastic exercises so that the gallant deeds of our forefathers and friends should early be implanted on the mind of the pupil'.[85] This interest in the town's turbulent history was dramatically intensified by the approach of the centenary of the siege. The moving spirit in the centenary celebrations was George Douglas, a Scotsman who edited the *Londonderry Journal* from 1772 to 1796. Douglas was responsible for the republication of Walker's *True Account* (1787), the diary of Captain Thomas Ash (1792), and an important collection of siege documents entitled *Derriana* (1793).[86] In 1788 he also offered a silver medal for the best poem on the siege, and received fifteen entries from Belfast, Hillsborough, Dromore, Ballymoney, the Maze, Coagh, Strabane

---

84 Quoted in Peter Smyth, '"Our Cloud-Cap't Grenadiers": The Volunteers as a Military Force', *Irish Sword*, XIII (1978-9), p. 204.

85 James Caldwell, 'Particulars of a North County Irish Family', PRONI, T.3541/5/3, p. 4.

86 Thomas Ash, *A Circumstantial Account of the Siege of Londonderry from a M.S. Written on the Spot and at the Time* (Londonderry, 1792); George Douglas (ed.), *Derriana—A Collection of Papers relative to the Siege of Derry, and Illustrative of the Revolution of 1688* (Londonderry, 1794).

and Derry.[87] In the same year, encouraged perhaps by the public dinners, processions and parties held in London and many English provincial towns to mark the centenary of William III's landing at Torbay, he assisted in the preparations for the most spectacular festival the citizens of Derry had ever witnessed.[88]

The centenary of the shutting of the gates—7 December 1788—was ushered in with the ringing of bells, the beating of drums, and the discharge of the cannon used in 1689; the red flag was displayed on the cathedral. At 10:30 a large procession left the Ship Quay, consisting of the corporation, the clergy, the naval officers and the 46th regiment, the Volunteers, the merchants and principal citizens, the merchants' apprentices, the tradesmen's apprentices, the young gentlemen of the Free School and the masters of ships and the seamen. Orange ribbons were universally worn. Anniversary sermons were preached in the cathedral by the Rev. John Hume, the dean of Derry, and in the First Presbyterian meeting-house by the Rev. Robert Black. At 2:00 p.m. the Volunteers and regular soldiers paraded, the gates were ceremonially closed, and there were *feux de joye* in the Diamond before a dinner in the town hall. Festivities continued the following day with the distribution of meat, bread and beer to the poor, and a ball.[89] Another elaborate spectacle was staged to mark the raising of the siege in August 1789, when the first stone of a triumphal arch, paid for by the corporation and the Irish Society, was laid.[90]

87   See *The Poliorciad, or Poems of the Siege* (Derry, 1789), reprinted in Douglas (ed.), *Derriana*. See also Rev. James Glass, *Libertas. A Poem* (Belfast, 1789); Rev. George Alley, *The Siege of Derry. A Poem* (Dublin, 1792).

88   Wilson, 'Inventing Revolution', pp. 354-7; Lois G. Schwoerer, 'Celebrating the Glorious Revolution', *Albion*, XXII (1990), pp. 3-8.

89   Douglas, 'Poliorciad', pp. 62-67.

90   Robert Simpson, *The Annals of Derry, Showing the Rise and Progress of the Town from the Earliest Accounts on Record to the Plantation under King James I—1613. And thence of the City of Londonderry to the Present Time* (Derry, 1847), pp. 186, 246.

These civic entertainments followed the pattern of the Glorious Revolution centenary in England, where great cities and county towns had witnessed similar displays of Orange ribbons, banners and flags, fireworks, pageantry, bell-ringing, speech-making and gunfire. In the Irish context, however, two aspects of the siege centenary deserve particular notice. On the hundredth anniversary of the shutting of the gates the official procession was imitated by 'the lower class of Citizens', who carried an effigy of Lundy through the streets and burned it in the market place 'with every circumstance of ignominy'.[91] This was the inauguration of one of the most vital rituals in the liturgy of Ulster loyalism which, unlike Guy Fawkes Night, has retained its political edge to the present day. In the later nineteenth century, when parades were banned under public order legislation, the Apprentice Boys Clubs would go to extraordinary lengths to conceal the effigy from the authorities until it could be despatched to the flames at dusk. The ritual was even observed on the western front towards the end of 1915, when members of the Ulster Division held a torchlit procession, accompanied by Orange music, and set fire to two straw figures of Lundy.[92]

The second remarkable feature of the centenary was the participation of the Roman Catholic clergy. 'Religious dissension', it was observed, 'seemed to be buried in oblivion, and Roman Catholics vied with Protestants in expressing, by every possible mark, their sense of the blessings secured to them by our happy Constitution'.[93] The rise of the Volunteers had brought a softening of the traditional hostility to Catholicism, and at the great Dungannon convention of 1782 the Ulster corps had welcomed the relaxation of the penal code. But Volunteer liberalism stopped well short of full emancipation: at a meeting of the Derry companies in August 1784 a resolution proposing the extension of the

91 Douglas, 'Poliorciad', p. 65.
92 Philip Orr, *The Road to the Somme: Men of the Ulster Division Tell Their Story* (Belfast, 1987), p. 116.
93 Douglas, 'Poliorciad', p. 65.

suffrage to Catholics had to be withdrawn.[94] After the French Revolution the Patriot tradition was fatally split between those who sought to reinterpret 1688 in the light of 1789, and those who attempted to reassert the powerful current of anti-Catholicism in British whiggery. On the one hand, the United Irishmen began to distance themselves from Williamite iconography, adopting new revolutionary symbols such as green ribbons and the cap of liberty; on the other, the Orange Order began to celebrate the Battle of the Boyne each 12 July as a symbolic affirmation of Protestant Ascendancy in Ireland.

The United Irish organisation was strong in County Londonderry, and there were signs of a new radicalism emerging within the Maiden City itself. A Whig Club was founded in 1790; a Derry edition of Paine's *Rights of Man* was issued the following year; and the city found its radical voice in the 'violent anti-ministerialist', the Rev. George Vaughan Sampson, an Anglican clergyman and the father of the United Irish leader William Sampson.[95] In the 1790 election the wealthy merchant William Lecky, backed by reformist sentiment, was elected to one of the two borough seats.[96] After his victory was announced, Lecky was carried through the town in a chair made from the old city gates, decorated with a green flag, the Irish harp, a wreath of shamrocks and the motto 'The Relief of Derry, 1790'—an interesting mixture of orange and green iconography which was not

---

94 Earl of Charlemont to Dr Alexander Haliday, 27 Aug. 1784, *The Manuscripts and Correspondence of James, First Earl of Charlemont*, 2 vols., HMC, 13th report, app. pt. VIII (1894), p. 6.

95 See [George Vaughan Sampson] *Remarks on the Present State of the Catholic Question in Ireland. Addressed to the Provost and Fellows of Trinity College. By a Clergyman of the Church of England, Member of the Royal Irish Academy, and Citizen of London-Derry* (Belfast, 1793). For the quotation see Jacques Louis Bougrenet, Chevalier De Latocnaye, *A Frenchman's Walk Through Ireland*, trans. John Stevenson (Belfast, 1917), p. 202.

96 Desmond Murphy, *Derry, Donegal and Modern Ulster 1790-1921* (Culmore, 1981), pp. 5-7.

at all incongruous in the context of eighteenth-century Irish Patriotism.[97] At a meeting held to mark the second anniversary of the storming of the Bastille, resolutions were passed comparing the heroic action of the Paris citizens with the patriotic spirit exhibited by the Apprentice Boys one hundred years before.[98] Unlike Belfast, however, Derry did not become a centre of radical politics. An attempt to establish a mixed company of Londonderry Union Volunteers was unsuccessful, and when the citizens met to elect delegates to the Dungannon reform convention of 1793 both Dean John Hume and the Rev. Robert Black counselled moderation.[99] Derry opinion supported the Act of Union of 1800, and Castlereagh referred to the city as 'the counterpoise to Belfast, and the rallying point for the loyalty of the north'.[100]

In the later 1790s Derry once more became a garrison city as the United Irish system spread through Counties Londonderry and Donegal, while government forces attempted to disarm the rebels. 'There is not a single Village', complained one magistrate, 'nay not even half a dozen Cabins together in this and many of the adjacent Counties' in which regular United Irish meetings were not held.[101] By March 1797 Sir George F. Hill believed that the two counties were practically in a state of insurrection, with fresh outrages reported every night; only decisive military action, he warned, could save situation.[102] Domestic disaffection fed on

---

97 Hempton (ed.), *Siege and History of Londonderry*, p. 426.
98 *Belfast News-Letter*, 26 July 1791; Hempton (ed.), *Siege and History of Londonderry*, p. 427.
99 Ibid., pp. 429-30.
100 *Memoirs and Correspondence of Viscount Castlereagh*, ed. Charles Vane, 3rd Marquis of Londonderry (12 vols., London, 1848-54), II, p. 33. See also Hill to Robert Peel, 17 Mar. 1816, PRONI, Hill Papers, D.642/22.
101 Rev. Isaac Ashe to Sackville Hamilton, 27 Jan. 1796, National Archives of Ireland [hereafter NAI], Rebellion Papers, 620/23/14.
102 Hill to Thomas Pelham, 20 March 1797, NAI, Rebellion Papers, 620/29/96 .

the danger of French invasion. When measures were taken for the defence of the city against the expected French landing at the end of 1796, Hill reported to Dublin Castle that 975 citizens were capable of bearing arms but that the walls could not be defended against cannon.[103] In 1797 the city gates were ordered to be shut at 9:00 each night.[104]

The disintegration of Ulster society in the 1790s, set against the background of war in Europe, inevitably altered the character of the siege celebrations. In December 1793, when the shutting of the gates was not celebrated, the *Londonderry Journal* felt it necessary to remind its readers that the anniversary stood not for 'sectarian prejudices' but for 'the broad principles of general good and well regulated liberty'.[105] After 1796 the Yeomanry, the militia and the regular troops put on a show of strength at each anniversary.[106] Until 1811 the Yeomanry, commanded by Sir George Hill, continued to parade along the walls, firing volleys not in the Diamond but over the gates to the accompaniment of 'loyal tunes'.[107] In parts of Ulster, as in Britain, the 1790s thus witnessed a conservative reaction against the threat of revolution. At the same time, the '98 rebellion—interpreted by Protestants as a popish conspiracy—quickly reawakened memories of 1641 and 1689. The language of patriotism, associated throughout the eighteenth century with parliamentary reform and opposition to government corruption, was giving way to the language of loyalism, an uncritical reverence for crown, church and constitution. As the citizens of Derry commemorated the shutting of the gates in 1798 the mayor rejoiced that

103 Hill to Edward Cooke, 27 Dec. 1796, NAI, Rebellion Papers, 620/26/165.
104 Hempton (ed.), *Siege and History of Londonderry*, p. 433.
105 *Londonderry Journal*, 10 Dec. 1793.
106 Hempton (ed.), *Siege and History of Londonderry*, pp. 432-5.
107 Ibid., pp. 435-40.

the same loyalty, for our King and love for our happy Constitution which glowed in the bosoms of our ancestors, is still ready to burst forth, on every occasion, at the call of danger. The sparks of liberty, loyalty and patriotism have been kept alive in this our MAIDEN CITY.[108]

IV

In the eighteenth century Derry was still a Protestant city. It was not until 1784 that a church was constructed for the small Catholic community outside the western walls. Relations between the different sects were generally good at this time, as we have seen, and the Catholics received generous donations from the corporation and from Frederick Augustus Hervey, Anglican bishop of Derry, best remembered for his outspoken support for both parliamentary reform and Catholic emancipation.[109] In the decades after the Act of Union, however, the denominational balance was transformed by an influx of Catholics from Donegal into the Bogside district and the religious geography of the modern city began to take shape. Writing in 1812, Edward Wakefield put the population of the town and suburbs at 10,000: Anglicans made up 1,600, Catholics, 3,500, and Dissenters the remainder. Although the town was still strongly Presbyterian, Wakefield remarked upon the extraordinary increase of Roman Catholics.[110] By 1834 the population had almost doubled to 19,000, with Catholics now forming nearly half of the population; by 1851 they already constituted a clear majority.[111] Like

108 Ibid., p. 435.
109 *Londonderry Journal*, 22 June 1784.
110 Edward Wakefield, *An Account of Ireland, Statistical and Political* (2 vols., London, 1812), II, p. 616.
111 Brian Lacy, *Siege City: The Story of Derry and Londonderry* (Belfast, 1990), p. 169.

Belfast, Derry expanded along lines of religious segregation, replicating the ethnic frontiers which carved up the Ulster countryside, and the struggle for territorial domination expressed itself in the annual parades organised by both communities.

For each of the three major denominations in Ulster, the opening decades of the nineteenth century was a period of internal reform and expansion. The rapid increase and greater visibility of Roman Catholic chapels coincided with the rise of an evangelical impulse within the Protestant churches to produce a new atmosphere of distrust in which relations between the Protestant and Catholic clergy deteriorated. The Catholic priesthood was politicised as Daniel O'Connell harnessed clerical aspirations, middle class frustration and rural discontent to his nationwide campaign for Catholic emancipation. When it became evident that British governments could no longer be trusted to uphold Protestant privileges, the Protestant population was mobilised for the first time. The forces of evangelical orthodoxy and political conservatism intersected in the Presbyterian clergyman and populist orator Henry Cooke. At a conservative demonstration in 1834—the same year that the first reliable census revealed that Irish Protestants were outnumbered by four to one—he issued his famous call for a 'platform of common Protestantism' to resist the further advance of the Church of Rome.[112] It comes as no surprise to find that Cooke, who took great pride in the fact that one of his ancestors had been in Derry during the siege, derived his model of pan-Protestant action from 1689.[113]

In the Maiden City the first signs of a new sectarian rift appeared in the years 1811-13, the first highpoint in Daniel O'Connell's emancipation crusade.[114] A large Catholic demon-

112 David Hempton and Myrtle Hill, *Evangelical Protestantism in Ulster Society 1740-1890* (London, 1992), p. 98.
113 Finlay Holmes, *Henry Cooke* (Belfast, 1981), pp. 115, 148.
114 For background information see Oliver Rafferty, 'Catholic and Protestant Relations in Derry in the Episcopacy of Charles O'Donnell, 1798-1823',

stration held in the town in 1811 announced the arrival of the Catholics as a political force, and two years later Father Cornelius O'Mullan, an O'Connellite who had ties with the underground lodges of the Ribbonmen, was imprisoned following a riot in the Roman Catholic chapel. At the same time the first objections to the siege celebrations were voiced. The annual parades had become more military in character; Orange regalia was now worn; and an Orange flag was flown over Cathedral. In 1811 seven Catholic members of the Londonderry Yeomanry were dismissed when they complained about the wearing of Orange lilies during the Relief commemoration.[115] In the surrounding countryside sectarian tensions had peaked as Orangemen and Ribbonmen clashed throughout County Londonderry.[116]

It is surely no coincidence that the Apprentice Boys organisation dates from 1813, the year the first motion for emancipation was passed by the British House of Commons. Although the movement has always been centred on Derry itself, the first club was actually formed in Dublin, on 7 December.[117] This 'numer-

---

Derriana: The Journal of the Derry Diocesan Historical Society, forthcoming. I am grateful to the author for allowing me to see an early version of this paper. Belfast's first sectarian riots also took place in 1813: see [John Hancock] Trial of the Belfast Orangemen (Belfast, 1813).

115 Hempton (ed.), Siege and History of Londonderry, pp. 440-1, 443-5.

116 Sir William Smith to Captain Cardew, forwarded by Major-General Fryers to Dublin castle, 17 Dec. 1813, NAI, SOC 1537/37; Rev. John Graham, 'A Journal of the Riots in the Neighbourhood of Maghera County of Londonderry. From April the 19th to July 26th 1813', NAI, SOC 1537/29.

117 [Sibbett], Orangeism, p. 192. The club was founded by fourteen Derrymen and membership was confined to freemen of the city and representatives of families who were or had been resident there. Early members included the bishop of Down, Lord Caledon and the magistrates George Hill and Henry Alexander. In 1817 they were joined by Lieutenant-Colonel William Blacker (1777-1855), a well known member of the Armagh gentry who had played a leading part in the creation of the Orange Order. The club continued to meet throughout the nineteenth century, dressing in leather aprons, dining, drinking Tory toasts and singing loyal songs; in

ous and highly respectable Society', made up of descendants of those who had defended Derry in 1689, assembled annually in Morrison's hotel, wearing medals engraved with Walker's image.[118] The Dublin association was described as an Irish equivalent of the Pitt Club, an indication of the political character which marked the organisation from its inception.[119] A Derry branch soon followed,[120] its foundation perhaps connected to a meeting of the freemen and freeholders held on 8 February 1814, which had drawn up an address condemning the Dublin Catholic Board.[121]

In the 1820s, as the government assumed a more neutral stance in Irish politics, the state began to withdraw its support from the Williamite celebrations. Both the Yeomanry and the regular troops had taken part in the siege parades until 1821, when the garrison was prevented from participating by its commanding officer, one Colonel Pearson. Protestant citizens defiantly formed themselves into companies and fired off the traditional volleys over the Gates and in the Diamond. Once more the political dimension of the anniversaries was made explicit. On 1 August 1822 George Dawson, M.P., made an attack on the radical press and on Jacobinism, while on 7 December 1822 the Rev. John Graham ridiculed the 'half-educated Ecclesiastics and blundering Demagogues' of the Roman Catholic Church.[122] The local

the later half of the century they held an annual procession bearing a plaster copy of Walker's skull. A collection of minute books and memorabilia can be found in the Robinson Library, Armagh.

118 Rev. John Graham, *Derriana, Consisting of a History of the Siege of Londonderry and Defence of Enniskillen, in 1688 and 1689, with Historical Poetry and Biographical Notes, &c.* (Londonderry, 1823), p. ii.

119 Ibid., p. ii.

120 Cecil Davis Milligan, *Browning Memorials (With a Short Historical Note on the Rise and Progress of the Apprentice Boys of Derry Clubs* (Londonderry, 1952), p. 12. Almost nothing known is known of this society except that a medal was struck in commemoration of Walker for its members in 1814: see ibid., p. 14.

121 Graham, *Derriana*, p. 160.

122 Ibid., pp. 156, 164.

Yeomanry appear to have participated in the street parades for a few more years, but with the formation of the No Surrender Club in 1824 the Apprentice Boys took control of the Derry rituals.[123]

Today the Apprentice Boys organisation is divided into eight parent clubs, with 245 branches in Ulster, Scotland, England, America, Canada and the Irish Republic. For several decades, however, the organisation had only a shaky existence, and the sketchy evidence that survives reveals a series of short-lived clubs appearing and disappearing from view.[124] The *Ordnance Survey* of 1837 listed three clubs, the first composed chiefly of old men, the No Surrender (1824), and the Death and Glory Club, recently founded by 'journeymen tradesmen'. These institutions were said to be losing influence and it was confidently predicted that they would become extinct.[125] By the middle of the century they had fallen into abeyance, but in their place there emerged a new wave of better organised associations—the Walker Club (1844), the Murray Club (1847), the Mitchelburne Club (1845, revived 1854), and the Browning Club (1854, revived 1876), and a central organisation, the General Committee of the Apprentice Boys, was formed in 1856 to co-ordinate the siege celebrations.

Unlike the civic processions of the eighteenth century, the parades organised by the Apprentice Boys since the early nineteenth century have no parallels in mainstream British culture. While the Orange Order is dedicated to the defence of the

---

123 Milligan, *Browning Memorials*, p. 12.
124 Information on the various clubs can be found in Cecil Davis Milligan, *The Murray Club Centenary: A Hundred Years of History of the Murray Club of Apprentice Boys of Derry, with the Story of Murray's part in the Defence of Derry in 1689* (Londonderry, 1947); idem, *Browning Memorials*; idem, *Mitchelburne Club*; W.J. Wallace, *Browning Club Apprentice Boys of Derry (1861-1961): A Brief History of the Club ... on the Occasion of the Centenary of its Revival* (Londonderry, 1961). Other clubs included the Fear Not Club, the Juvenile Club, the True Blue, the Williamite Club and the Cairnes Club.
125 Thomas Colby, *Ordnance Survey of the County Londonderry* (Dublin, 1837), pp. 197-8.

Protestant religion, the various Apprentice Boys Clubs exist sole-
ly for the purpose of commemorating the two siege anniversaries. Nevertheless, their processions, complete with regalia,
bands and banners, provide a characteristically Irish combination
of street theatre, religious observance and political demonstration.
Like the Twelfth of July marches they can be used to demarcate
the communal boundaries established by seventeenth-century
settlement, and to affirm symbolically the political and social
dominance of Protestants. The assertion of territorial claims
implicit in these processions is clear from the report of the Royal
Commission appointed to investigate the Derry riots of 1868. It
was found that the Protestants, sometimes aided by the police and
the military, had repeatedly opposed the attempts of Catholic
processions to storm the city gates, while the inhabitants of the
Bogside expressed a corresponding fear that Orangemen might
'violate their territory'.[126]

The Apprentice Boys Clubs, who numbered among their
members many prominent citizens, quickly became the recognised guardians of the siege myth. In the 1820s they mounted the
famous siege cannon 'Roaring Meg' on a carriage and used it for
salutes during the celebrations.[127] The shell thrown into the city
containing the Jacobite proposals for surrender was erected on a
stand in the vestibule of the Cathedral in 1844, and when bones
were discovered during the renovation of the cathedral in 1861,
the Apprentice Boys had them re-interred in the siege heroes'
mound in the graveyard.[128] The organisation was also responsible
for the erection of the most famous of all Derry monuments, the

126 Report of the Commissioners of Inquiry, 1869, into the Riots and Disturbances
   in the City of Londonderry, H.C., 1870, XXXII, pp. 12, 18. For the significance of parades in defining territorial boundaries, see D.W. Miller,
   Queen's Rebels: Ulster Loyalism in Historical Perspective (Dublin, 1978), pp.
   68-71; Desmond Bell, Acts of Union: Youth Culture and Sectarianism in
   Northern Ireland (Basingstoke, 1990).
127 Hempton (ed.), Siege and History of Londonderry, p. 446.
128 Ibid., pp. 450, 483.

Walker Testimonial, built at the expense of £4200 between 1826 and 1828.[129] Situated on the royal bastion—where the western city walls overlooked the Catholic Bogside—the monument consisted of an 81-foot column, with a spiral staircase up the inside of 110 steps, topped with a 9-foot statue of Walker. In his right hand he held a bible; in his left he originally brandished a sword, but this was blown down in a storm, as local tradition has it, on the day that Catholic emancipation was passed.[130]

The construction of the Walker Testimonial signalled a change in the meaning of the siege myth, a reversion to the cyclical interpretation of Irish history as a recurrent struggle between Popery and Protestantism. In a speech made on 7 December 1826, when the first stone was laid, James Gregg set out to prove that 'POPERY abstractedly considered, *ever was, now is,* and *ever will be* INCORRIGIBLY THE SAME'.[131] The '*perverted conciliation*' of Roman Catholicism was denounced and O'Connell's popular organisation compared to the threat posed by the native Irish in 1688.[132] By the early 1840s the Walker Testimonial had become the focal point of the siege celebrations: the Crimson flag was hoisted beside the statue, field pieces were discharged over the Catholic quarter below, and the ceremonial burning of Lundy had been moved from the Diamond to this more provocative location.[133] The monument was destroyed by an IRA bomb in 1973.[134]

After the prohibition of Orange parades by the Party Processions Act of 1832, several Apprentice Boys were prosecut-

---

129 Ibid., p. 447; Simpson, *Annals*, p. 247.

130 Richard Hayward, *In Praise of Ulster* (London, 1938), p. 260.

131 [James] Gregg, *The Apprentice Boys of Derry, and No Surrender! or, Protestant Heroism Triumphant over Popish Malignity; Being a Succinct and Interesting Account of the Siege of Derry* (London, 1827), p. 3.

132 Ibid., pp. 3, 5.

133 Colby, *Ordnance Survey*, p. 119, Hempton (ed.), *Siege and History of Londonderry*, p. 450.

134 It has since been replaced by a commemorative plinth.

ed, but the annual parades continued in modified form, without muskets or music, until the 1860s.[135] Despite occasional skirmishes between the Apprentice Boys and the local authorities, Derry escaped the fierce sectarian disturbances which erupted sporadically in Belfast during these years. The turning point came with the general election of 1868, in which the disestablishment of the Church of Ireland provided the central issue. The Reform Act of the previous year had produced an expanded Catholic electorate which initially bolstered the forces of Ulster Liberalism. In Derry an alliance of Presbyterian Liberals and Catholics enabled Richard Dowse Q.C. to unseat the Conservative Lord Claud Hamilton, earning him the nickname of 'member for Bogside'.[136] Until this election, recalled one prominent Derryman, the inhabitants had been 'peaceful, quiet, God-fearing folk'.[137] Over the next three years, however, a series of clashes occurred between the Apprentice Boys, and 'the Bogside or Catholic party', beginning with an attack on a Liberal meeting by an armed Protestant mob on 20 July 1868.[138]

The Apprentice Boys parades had met with occasional opposition since the 1830s, as a wide range of Catholic grievances became focused on the most visible symbols of Protestant superiority, but it was only with the formation of the Catholic Workingmen Defence Association in August 1869 that a policy of violent confrontation was adopted.[139] A year later a manifesto was issued calling on Roman Catholics to assemble in their thou-

135 Ibid., p. 449. The Party Processions Act lapsed in 1845; another was passed in 1850 and repealed in 1872.
136 James Connor Doak, 'Rioting and Civil Strife in the City of Londonderry during the Nineteenth and Early Twentieth Centuries', M.A. thesis, Queen's University of Belfast, 1978, p. 127. I have made extensive use of this thesis in my account of nineteenth-century Derry.
137 Sir John Ross, *The Years of My Pilgrimage* (London, 1924), p. 11.
138 The details can be found in Doak, 'Rioting and Civil Strife', ch. 3. The quotation is from the *Report of the Commissioners of Inquiry, 1869*, p. 12.
139 Murphy, *Derry, Donegal and Modern Ulster*, pp. 49-50, 56-7, 116, 120.

sands to prevent the annual Relief procession; the government responded by sending 1,000 infantry, 1,000 police and 100 carbineers to the city and by cancelling the local trains.[140] By this stage the Presbyterian Liberals had also distanced themselves from the August and December parades. Only ten years before, the leading Liberal, William McClure, had preached Relief anniversary sermons, marked less by anti-Catholicism than by the high-minded evangelical fervour that characterised Derry Liberalism.[141] In 1864, however, the committee of the First Presbyterian Congregation refused the Mitchelburne Club use of their meeting-house because they objected to party colours and flags. The General Committee of Apprentice Boys retaliated with shrill warnings about the principles of 1798, a reminder of the chasm which still separated the two Protestant churches.[142] Presbyterian opposition to the siege anniversaries was stimulated by the increasingly partisan complexion assumed by the Apprentice Boys, as Lord Claud Hamilton sought to use the organisation as a vehicle for the Tory-Episcopalian party in the town.[143] In

140 Aiken McClelland, *William Johnston of Ballykilbeg* (Lurgan, 1990), p. 72.

141 For McClure the besiegers were not the Irish Catholics but the forces of darkness generally: 'And when you think of the achievements of our venerated fathers ... remember you are engaged in a conflict with enemies more formidable than those who tried to scale our city walls, but to whom they would never surrender—you contend with sin, and Satan, and the world': see his *Sermon ... on the Twelfth of August, 1859*, p. 4. See also idem, *A Sermon Preached in the First Presbyterian Church of Londonderry, on Monday, the 12th of August, 1861, Being the 171st [sic] Anniversary of the Relief of that City* (Londonderry, 1861).

142 James Crawford, *Alleluia: The Commemoration Sermon, Preached on 12 August, 1864, the 175th Anniversary of the Relief of Londonderry, in the Strand Presbyterian Church* (Londonderry, 1864), p. 15.

143 Murphy, *Derry, Donegal and Modern Ulster*, p. 116. After the Apprentice Boys celebrated the marriage of the Prince of Wales in 1863, the Mitchelburne Club withdrew from the General Committee feeling it necessary to point out that the local anniversaries should not be involved in 'any political complication': Francis J. Porter, *Be In Earnest: A Sermon, Delivered before the Mitchelburne Club, on 12 August, 1863, Anniversary of the*

December 1865 the *Londonderry Standard* protested that the parades had degenerated into Conservative party rallies.[144] The shutting of the gates ceremony was banned five years later, a policy maintained until the Party Processions Act was repealed in 1872, after the Belfast M.P. William Johnston had raised the issue of the siege celebrations in the House of Commons.[145]

A distinct change in the tone of the Derry celebrations was by now evident, as the constitutional aspects of the Williamite revolution were relegated in favour of its religious significance. It was not whig principles which led the apprentices to close the gates, declared one Protestant spokesman, but fears of a popish massacre: 'the true meaning of the commemorations' was that 'the Protestant religion was preserved'.[146] It was scarcely surprising, then, that the Royal Commissioners of 1869 discovered that the vast majority of Roman Catholics now looked on the celebrations as offensive.[147] As the numbers attending the parades had multiplied, so Catholic resentment had hardened. An earlier Royal Commission noted the convergence of Protestants from Derry, Donegal and Tyrone each August and December, concluding that the celebrations, once possessed of 'merely local associations' were now occasions for 'a public demonstration of physical strength'.[148] The problem was exacerbated by the construction of new railway lines which linked Derry to the major towns of the north-west in 1847 and to the north-east in 1853.

Relief of Londonderry. With an Appendix, Historical Epitome, Rules, &c., of the Mitchelburne Club (Derry, 1863), pp. 21-2. The Mitchelburne Club also disclaimed the practice of affiliating members from other parts of the UK and colonies.

144 Doak, 'Rioting and Civil Strife', p. 100.

145 McClelland, *Johnston of Ballykilbeg*, p. 73.

146 Verax, *The Derry Celebrations: Being a Series of Letters, Written for the Londonderry Sentinel in Reply to Some Editorials Published in the Londonderry Standard* (Derry, 1871), pp. 9-10.

147 *Report of the Commissioners of Inquiry, 1869*, p. 16.

148 *First Report of the Commissioners Appointed to Inquire into Municipal Corporations in Ireland (23)*, H.C., 1835, XXVII, p. 1.

In the emergence of Protestant Ulster's famous siege mentality, however, it is again the Liberal assault on the Church of Ireland which stands out as the decisive moment. The campaign for disestablishment was viewed as an unholy conspiracy of Ultramontanes, Ritualists, secularists and Voluntaries. Conservative leaders warned that the abolition of the state church would lead inexorably to the repeal of the union and to papal supremacy. On 17 April 1868 the Londonderry Working Men's Protestant Defence Association was formed, with the objective of uniting Protestants of every denomination in defence of the Protestant churches of the empire and encouraging loyalty to the throne. The society was pledged to oppose all schemes for the endowment of popery and resist all efforts by the Church of Rome to obtain control over education provided by the state.[149] Its president, the local architect John Guy Ferguson, was also governor of the Apprentice Boys.

At the inaugural meeting of the Association, the Rev. Richard Babington invoked the spirit of the thirteen apprentices, advising his listeners to 'Sink all those differences which have too often disunited the Protestants of this country, and in this, the hour of your country's danger, stand shoulder to shoulder, and contend manfully, for your privileges, your rights.'[150] At the same meeting a lecture on 'The Duty of Protestants', delivered by the well known Orange chief, Stewart Blacker, harked back to the 'beleaguered city' of 1688, when 'men of all Churches, men of all creeds' had stood together on the ancient walls and raised the cry of 'No Surrender'.[151] This siege symbolism was continued at the next meeting, when the Rev. John Bryson identified Gladstone as a latter-day Lundy.[152] The most notorious Protestant preacher

149 *Londonderry Working Men's Protestant Defence Association. Report of Inaugural Meeting, &c., Held on Friday, 17th April, 1868* (Derry, 1868), p. iii.
150 Ibid., p. 3.
151 Ibid., p. 26.
152 John Bryson, *An Address delivered in the Corporation Hall, Londonderry, on Wednesday Evening, May 20, 1868* (Derry and Belfast, 1868), p. 17.

of this period, 'Roaring' Hugh Hanna of Belfast, also employed the siege myth in his efforts to minimise differences between Presbyterians and Episcopalians and to strengthen loyalist solidarity. In a lecture given in Broughshane in 1871, Hanna rehearsed the story of 1688 and 1689, concluding succinctly that '"Protestant Union", the more effectually to resist the aggression of Papacy, was the moral of it.'[153] The perceived weakness of the British government in the face of Roman Catholic aggression thus created the conditions in which the siege began to serve its modern function in Protestant rhetoric.

Both Hugh Hanna and John Bryson, it should be noted, were Presbyterians. Their sentiments were echoed by a growing number of non-conformist clergymen prepared to throw their weight behind their old oppressor, the established church. In Derry, as the 1868 election had demonstrated, Episcopalians and Roman Catholics voted fairly solidly for the Conservatives and the Liberals respectively, while the Presbyterians remained divided.[154] The mobilisation of the Liberal electorate depended on an alliance of Catholic priests and Presbyterian clergymen, and Claud Hamilton had attributed his defeat to the influence of several Dissenting ministers.[155] Liberalism, however, is best viewed as a transitional stage in Ulster politics, a unique product of the period between the creation of a large Catholic electorate in 1868 and the emergence of an independent Catholic leadership.

153 Hugh Hanna, *Weighed and Wanting. An Examination by the Rev. Hugh Hanna of a Review by the Rev. Archibald Robinson, of a Lecture on 'The Siege of Derry'*, *by the Rev. Hugh Hanna* (Belfast, 1871), p. 13. This pamphlet demonstrates clearly the differences between Conservative and Liberal Presbyterian interpretations of the siege. See also Hugh Hanna, *'A Memorial of the Divine Mercies to our Fathers', Being a Sermon Delivered to the Apprentice Boys, in the Strand Presbyterian Church, on 12th August, 1863, the 174th Anniversary of Derry's Deliverance* (Derry, 1863), pp. 15-17.

154 For a denominational breakdown of the voting figures in the 1868 election, see B.M. Walker, *Ulster Politics: The Formative Years, 1868-86* (Belfast, 1989), p. 63.

155 Walker, *Ulster Politics*, p. 62.

The Liberal coalition was shaken in 1872, when a large section of Presbyterians deserted to the Tories and a Home Rule candidate was fielded for the first time.[156] The unstable alliance of Presbyterian tenant farmers and middle-class Catholics could not survive the emergence of confessional politics in 1880s.

V

Just as the first accounts of the Siege of Derry had been coloured by the schism between the Church of Ireland and the Synod of Ulster, so the historiography of the nineteenth century was shaped by the very different party and sectarian rivalries which emerged after the Act of Union. In 1823 a sober, detailed history of the siege was published by Joshua Gillespie, one time mayor of Derry and member of the Apprentice Boys, and dedicated to Sir George Hill.[157] More partisan was Charlotte Elizabeth Phelan's *Derry, A Tale of the Revolution of 1688* (1833), a semi-fictional presentation of the siege which ridiculed Catholic superstition, highlighted popish cruelty, and urged the lesson that 'Popery will always be the same'.[158] In 1861 the memoirs of Walker, Mackenzie and Ash were gathered together with a history of Derry in a compendium by John Hempton, president of the Mitchelburne Club.[159]

In the popularisation of the siege myth, however, the most important local historian was the Rev. John Graham (1776–1844), Anglican curate of Lifford and later rector of Magilligan on

---

156 Ibid., p. 83.
157 Joshua Gillespie, *A Narrative of the Most Remarkable Events in the Life of William the Third King of England, and Prince of Orange. Also, a Revised History of the Siege of Londonderry* (Derry, 1823).
158 Charlotte Elizabeth Phelan [afterwards Tonna], *Derry, A Tale of the Revolution of 1688* (London, 1833), p. xv. By 1839 this book had already gone through six editions.
159 John Hempton (ed.), *Siege and History of Londonderry* (Londonderry, Dublin, London, 1861).

the coast of County Londonderry. As a boy he had witnessed the centenary celebration of 1788, and his poems, including 'The Shutting of the Gates' (1821) became so well known in Ulster 'as to be included at almost every loyal fireside amongst the household words'.[160] Graham had involved himself in the theological disputes of the 'second reformation',[161] and his career as a Williamite orator culminated in his appointment as senior chaplain of the Grand Orange Lodge of Ireland. His historical investigations began with his *Annals of Ireland, Ecclesiastical, Civil and Military* (London, 1819), a large collection of 'tragical documents' from the 1640s, designed to demonstrate the persecuting spirit of the papists.[162] From then onwards he concentrated on the siege. His major work, *Derriana, Consisting of a History of the Siege of Londonderry and Defence of Enniskillen* was published in 1823 along with a collection of his poems on the siege; a second edition followed in 1829.[163] As we have already seen, Graham was a moving spirit in the early Apprentice Boys organisation, and his anti-Catholic interpretation of the siege should be seen in the context of the Protestant backlash against the emancipation movement. The actions of the defenders of Derry, in his view, had enabled

160 Rev. John Graham, *Ireland Preserved; or the Siege of Londonderry and Battle of Aughrim, with Lyrical Poems and Biographical Notes* (Dublin, 1841), p. x.

161 Alexander James M'Carron, *Refutation of Mr Hayden's Vindication of his Speech: Proving that he has Neither Vindicated his Speech, nor Refuted my Pamphlet* (Derry, 1827), pp. 77–80.

162 Rev. John Graham, *Annals of Ireland, Ecclesiastical, Civil and Military* (London, 1819), p. 258.

163 Rev. John Graham, *Derriana, Consisting of a History of the Siege of Londonderry and Defence of Enniskillen, in 1688 and 1689, with Historical Poetry and Biographical Notes, &c.* (Londonderry, 1823); idem, *A History of the Siege of Derry and Defence of Enniskillen in 1688 and 1689* (2nd edn., Dublin, 1829). See also idem, *Memoirs of the Rev. George Walker, D.D. Governour of Derry, and of Colonel David Cairnes of Knockmany, Defenders of the City in 1689* (Newtownlimavady, 1832); idem, *A History of Ireland, from the Relief of Londonderry in 1689 to the Surrender of Limerick in 1691* (Dublin, 1839); idem, *Ireland Preserved; or the Siege of Londonderry and Battle of Aughrim, with Lyrical Poems and Biographical Notes* (Dublin, 1841).

every man to worship God as his light, and knowledge, and conscience instruct him—an independent being—free to think, free to speak, free to act upon the spontaneous dictates of his judgement—the slave of no system—the creature of no tyrant.[164]

Graham's popular narratives, poems and sermons introduced the heroes of 1689 to a wider audience than ever before. But the most influential contribution to siege historiography was made not by a Derryman, but by Macaulay's epic *History of England from the Accession of James the Second* (1848-55), perhaps the most celebrated work of English history of all time. Often regarded as the chief exemplar of the whig interpretation of history, Macaulay located the central thread of English experience in the gradual triumph of constitutional liberty and representative government.[165] In the evolution of English liberty from Magna Carta to limited monarchy and the rule of law it was the Glorious Revolution which provided the real landmark in sorting out the relationship between crown and parliament, and King William was the hero of Macaulay's work. More than any other single text, Macaulay's brief, vivid description of the Siege of Derry strengthened the emotional and historical links between Great Britain and the Protestants of Ulster, achieving a massive public relations *coup* for the loyalist cause. The first two volumes, which appeared in December 1848, were an instant runaway success; by March 1849 they had sold 13,000 copies in Britain, and American sales were reaching 100,000.[166] When the third and fourth volumes appeared in 1855 Longmans took advance orders

164 Graham, 'Extract from a Sermon on the Relief of Londonderry, 1689', 12 August 1838, in ibid., p. 265.
165 Owen Dudley Edwards, *Macaulay* (London, 1988); John Clive, *Thomas Babington Macaulay: The Shaping of the Historian* (1976); J.W. Burrow, *A Liberal Descent: Victorian Historians and the English Past* (Cambridge, 1981).
166 Edwards, *Macaulay*, p. 50.

for 25,000 copies. Since then the book has never been out of print.[167]

The *History of England* gave Ulster Protestants a central place in the myth of the unfolding British constitution, and the book is still quoted by Unionists to show Ulster's importance in the struggle for civil and religious liberty, for representative institutions and ultimately for democracy itself.[168] Macaulay had spent two days in Derry at the end of August 1849, when he had learned of local traditions from the inhabitants, sketched a groundplan of the streets and made a circuit of the walls four times.[169] Indebted to the novels of Sir Walter Scott as well as Tacitus and Thucydides, the resulting description of the siege is regarded as one of his finest passages. Only a few years after its publication Macaulay's *History* was being plagiarised by James Edward Finlay, editor of the *Londonderry Sentinel*, in an attack on the Liberal government which described the place of the defenders of Derry in securing prosperity, education, literature and science, the Bill of Rights, Habeas Corpus, freedom of the press and liberty of conscience.[170]

But there is an irony in Ulster's encounter with whig historiography. Macaulay's *History* was not whig in a narrowly partisan sense; the reason for its astounding success lay in its encapsulation of certain fundamental assumptions about the English national character. For his Victorian readership, the Stuart period—for so long the test of party politics—was losing its relevance as the rela-

167 John Kenyon, *The History Men: The Historical Profession in England since the Renaissance* (2nd edition, London, 1993), pp. 75-6.
168 Gordon Lucy (ed.), *Macaulay on Londonderry, Enniskillen and the Boyne* (Tandragee, 1989). On the reception of Macaulay in Ulster, see James Loughlin, *Ulster Unionism and British National Identity since 1885* (London, 1995), pp. 15, 24-6.
169 George Otto Trevelyan, *The Life and Labours of Lord Macaulay* (enlarged edition, London, 1908), p. 499.
170 James Edward Finlay, *The Siege of Londonderry: Compiled from the Best Sources* (2nd edition, Londonderry, 1861), pp. 31-2. The first edition was published in 1860, but I have been unable to find a copy.

tionship between crown and parliament and the conflict between Church and non-conformity were replaced by alignments based more clearly on class. Only the Irish question, which still possessed the power to shape party alignments at Westminster, continued to supply seventeenth-century conflicts with a contemporary bite; Macaulay himself remarked that to write of Ireland was to tread on a volcano whose lava was still glowing.[171] Even as Ulster's valiant role in the British past was confirmed, its increasingly anomalous position in contemporary British society was thus exposed. It was difficult to reconcile the religious enthusiasm of Irish politics with the English genius for orderly, piecemeal reform.

These tensions are already present in Macaulay's work. In a short introduction, he was forced to admit that despite the material and intellectual achievements which followed 1688, Ireland, 'cursed by the domination of race over race, and of religion over religion', remained a reproach to England.[172] Macaulay was a constructive unionist *avant la lettre*, dedicated to the removal of religious inequalities, but implacably opposed to repeal.[173] When he came to discuss the character of the Protestant Ascendancy he was pulled in two contrary directions: 'Seen on one side, it must be regarded by every well constituted mind with disapprobation. Seen on the other, it irresistibly extorts applause.'[174] Although he disapproved of the arrogance of the Protestants, and condemned the 'hateful laws' which 'disgraced the Irish statute book', he

171 J.W. Burrow, *A Liberal Descent: Victorian Historians and the English Past* (Cambridge, 1981), p. 16.

172 Macaulay, *History of England*, I, p. 2.

173 In a speech against repeal Macaulay had put forward the novel argument that if Catholic Ireland deserved its own parliament in Dublin, then Protestant Ulster ought to have one in Londonderry: Thomas Babington Macaulay, *Repeal of the Union with Ireland: A Speech by Lord Macaulay, Delivered in the House of Commons on the 6th of February, 1833* (Dublin, 1886). p. 13.

174 Macaulay, *History of England*, III, p. 194.

could not help but admire their resolution in times 'of distress and peril'.[175] Similarly, he found himself in two minds on the subject of the Derry anniversaries. While he insisted that a people must take pride in the achievements of its ancestors, he regretted that 'the expressions of pious gratitude which have resounded from [Ulster's] pulpits have too often been mingled with words of wrath and defiance.'[176]

Before returning to Ulster writers, it is perhaps worth mentioning that there is also an American version of the siege myth. Among the first Presbyterian emigrants to the colonies had been a number of siege veterans, including the Rev. James McGregor and the Rev. Matthew Clerk, founders of the township of Londonderry in New Hampshire. Along with their political and religious principles, the linen industry and the potato, these settlers brought with them their historical myths and memories. During the war for American Independence, the Presbyterian clergy of Philadelphia cast George III in the role of James II, reminding their congregations of their ancestors' struggle for liberty at Derry and Enniskillen.[177] In the first half of the nineteenth century there was an upsurge of interest among Ulster-Americans in their 'Scotch-Irish' heritage, stimulated by the centenary celebrations of a number of New Hampshire towns and by the popularity of both Scottish philosophy and Sir Walter Scott. Above all, the Ulster-Americans were eager to dissociate themselves from the new tide of immigrants from Catholic Ireland. The first historians of Ulster emigration therefore stressed the Scottish origins of their ancestors, largely ignoring the Irish dimension. This omission was quickly rectified when American editions of both Macaulay's *History of England* and Graham's *History of the Siege of Londonderry* became available. Typical was Edward Parker's *History of Londonderry* (1851), which used the

175 Ibid., III, pp. 194-5.
176 Ibid., III, p. 241.
177 Kerby A. Miller, *Emigrants and Exiles: Ireland and the Irish Exodus to North America* (New York and Oxford, 1985), p. 166.

siege to demonstrate the 'the resolute, determined, unyielding spirit of Protestantism'.[178] For the historians of American Presbyterianism the rugged individualism of the Ulster pioneers had been forged in the fires of 1689, preparing them for their historic task of taming the American wilderness. The siege had become the definitive moment in the Scotch-Irish experience, the *locus classicus* of all those virtues which distinguished the old Ulster-American communities from the recent immigrant Irish. Isaac Barnes of Bedford, New Hampshire, made the point succinctly: 'The Scotch are zealous Protestants, and Presbyterians. The Irish as zealous Roman Catholics. The Scotch were the besieged, and the Irish the besiegers at Londonderry.'[179]

Just as American historians drew on Ulster history to bolster their ethnic identity, so Irish Presbyterians exploited the Scotch-Irish heritage when they came to define their own cultural tradition.[180] The close cultural links between the two countries were demonstrated when Thomas Witherow[181] dedicated his *Derry and Enniskillen in the Year 1689* (1873) to the Rev. William McClure,

178 Parker, *History of Londonderry ... N.H.*, pp. 7-28.

179 Quoted in Wallace, 'The Scotch-Irish of Provincial New Hampshire', p. 61. Much of the information in this paragraph has been drawn from this fascinating dissertation.

180 Two early examples are Thomas Croskery, 'Ulster and its People', *Frazer's Magazine*, XIV (1876), pp. 219-29 and idem, *Irish Presbyterianism: Its History, Character, Influence and Present Disposition* (Dublin, 1884), pp. 41-3. For the cultural construction of the Ulster Scot see Ian McBride, 'Ulster and the British Problem', in Richard English and Graham Walker (eds.), *Unionism in Modern Ireland* (Macmillan, 1996).

181 Thomas Witherow, born 1824, educated Belfast Academical Institution and Edinburgh; conversion experience 1842, licensed and ordained at Maghera 1845, professor of church history at Magee College, 1865; editor of the Liberal *Londonderry Standard* 1878-86; wrote widely in church history and controversial theology. Like other Presbyterian historians, Witherow took a strong anti-Walker line, and had contributed an article entitled 'Adam Murray, the Hero of the Siege' to the *Evangelical Witness* in 1878. Further biographical details can be found in Douglas Armstrong, *The Life and Work of the Rev. Prof. Thomas Witherow* (Belfast, 1985).

an honorary member of the Historical Society of New Hampshire.[182] Witherow, the last nineteenth-century historian to be considered here, had been taught the story of the siege at his grandmother's knee. His historical curiosity was reawakened by the documents republished by Killen and Hempton, by the appearance of Macaulay's *History of England*, and by his appointment to the chair of church history at Magee College, Derry.[183] Established as a Presbyterian seminary in 1865, Magee College was a focal point of Ulster Liberalism, and many of the most prominent Liberal spokesmen were associated with it at some stage in their careers.[184] In a college competition in 1867 one student had expressed the hope that his prize-winning poem on the siege would not rekindle 'that hot, anti-Popery spirit which characterized the exciting times of the English Revolution'.[185] Similarly Witherow, though he wrote from 'an entirely Protestant standpoint', aspired to an 'even-handed' approach which would 'rise superior to the passions of an evil age'.[186]

Derry and Enniskillen aimed to rescue the siege from the Orangemen and the Tories. William III emerges from its pages as a champion of religious toleration frustrated by the bigots of the established church. Witherow denounced the eighteenth-century penal code, arguing that if the Irish parliament had followed William's wishes, 'the likelihood is that all classes of the nation would, long ere this, have been welded together in a common

---

182 The book was reprinted 1875 and 1885; for its popularity see *The Autobiography of Thomas Witherow 1824-1890*, ed. Graham Mawhinney and Eull Dunlop (Draperstown, 1990), p. 121.

183 Ibid., p. 121.

184 Examples are the barrister J.J. Shaw and the Rev. Richard Smyth, professor of biblical criticism and Liberal M.P. for County Londonderry, 1874-8. For a brief history of the college see R.F.G. Holmes, *Magee 1865-1965: The Evolution of the Magee College* (Belfast, 1965).

185 Thomas Young, *The Siege of Derry. A Prize Poem in Four Cantos and Occasional Pieces* (Dublin and London, 1868), preface.

186 Witherow, *Derry and Enniskillen*, p. viii.

brotherhood'.[187] While conservative historians tended towards a cyclical view of history, underlining the need for constant vigilance against an unchanging Catholic threat, Witherow furnished an optimistic, progressive reading of the past, which took for granted the civilising benefits of British power. He emphasised the moral and material advances which had followed the Act of Union, looking forward to the day when the Irish would be released from the burden of their troubled past. Ireland was now part of a great empire where public office was open to all denominations: 'The days of privilege and exclusion are at an end, so far as it is in the power of law and government to end them'.[188] It was natural that Ulster Protestants should cherish the memories of their ancestors, who had contributed so powerfully to this unfolding of civil and religious liberty, but they should do so without causing provocation to their fellow countrymen:

> common sense must surely suggest how impolitic and discreditable it is, to adopt any form of commemoration of heroic acts, which is regarded by any section of our countrymen as an offence, and which reminds them of defeat and humiliation.[189]

Like Macaulay, Witherow viewed British history as an evolutionary process. He aimed to set the siege in the context of a more violent and unstable age and took it for granted that the civil war of 1688–89 was over. Events were soon to prove him wrong.

187 Ibid., pp. 241–50; quotation at p. 249.
188 Ibid., pp. 322–3.
189 Ibid., pp. 325–6, 330.

VI

In Derry the alliance of Presbyterian and Catholic, already under pressure in 1872, collapsed in the elections of 1885-6. The polarisation of Ulster politics had begun with the 'invasion of Ulster' launched by the Home Rule party in 1883. In a by-election held in June, the Parnellite Timothy Healy had been returned for Co. Monaghan; later in the year National League meetings clashed with Orange counter-demonstrations in Rosslea, Omagh, Dungannon and Aughnacloy. At the relief of Derry celebrations in August a number of speakers made it plain that Ulster Protestantism was being put on a war footing. John Guy Ferguson, president of the Apprentice Boys, warned that 'the men of this northern outpost will be able to give a good account of themselves if ever the day of action should come'.[190] Another outburst of sectarian fighting, involving the use of firearms, followed in October, when the Apprentice Boys occupied the Corporation Hall to prevent a National League rally taking place. A Royal Commission set up to investigate the riots noted the participation of 'a number of gentlemen of position and influence', including Lord Ernest Hamilton, a foretaste of the cross-class alliance created to oppose Home Rule after 1886.[191]

The political realignment of the 1880s should be viewed against the background of what F.S.L. Lyons has called 'the nationalization of Irish politics'.[192] By the last quarter of the century the extension of the railway network had broken down the isolation of 'the black north'. The sectarian warfare which punctuated the history of nineteenth-century Belfast is often

190 *Derry Journal*, 15 August 1883, quoted in Doak, 'Rioting and Civil Strife', p. 167. The title of the *Londonderry Journal* was abbreviated in 1880 after it came under Nationalist ownership.
191 *Report of a Commission Appointed to Inquire into Certain Disturbances which Took Place in the City of Londonderry, on the 1st November, 1883*, H.C., 1884, XXXVIII, p. vi. See also the speech of Lord Ernest Hamilton, ibid., p. 84.
192 F.S.L. Lyons, *Culture and Anarchy in Ireland 1890-1939* (Oxford, 1979), p. 142.

explained as an expression of local socio-economic competition between Protestant and Catholic workers, but it also indicates the impact of national politics on the northern capital. The riots of 1841 were occasioned by Daniel O'Connell's visit; in 1864 eighteen days of disorder followed the laying of the foundation stone of the O'Connell monument in Dublin; the disturbances of 1886 were triggered by the passage of the Home Rule bill through the House of Commons. The crucial point here, as newspaper editor Thomas MacKnight noted, was the novel identification of Ulster Catholics with their brethren in the south, and an increasing awareness among Protestants of their minority position on the island of Ireland.[193]

The growth in communications was accompanied by the creation of a more democratic electoral system by the Third Reform Act of 1884. The general election of the following year established the pattern of electoral geography for the new age of mass politics. In the south the Home Rulers triumphed in every single constituency with the exception of Trinity College Dublin. Even in Ulster, nationalists took 17 seats, giving them a majority of one. After this election, as David Miller has observed, 'The province as a whole was invested with the sense of territoriality which the Orange Order and Protestant ghetto-dwellers had kept alive in the middle years of the century on the level of much smaller, more discrete, geographical units.'[194] As demographic divisions became more sharply defined, the sense of siege already evident in Derry became generalised: Protestant Ulster was shutting its gates.

The threat of Home Rule led to an increase in the employment of siege imagery in Protestant rhetoric. In 1886 William

193 Thomas MacKnight, *Ulster As It Is, or Twenty-Eight Years' Experience as an Irish Editor* (2 vols., London, 1896), I, pp. 33-5. For the Belfast riots, see F.F. Moore, *The Truth about Ulster* (London, 1917), chs. 1-3; Stewart, *Narrow Ground*, pp. 137-54; Fred Heatley, 'Community Relations and the Religious Geography 1800-86', in J.C. Beckett et al., *Belfast: The Making of the City 1800-1914* (Belfast, 1983), pp. 129-42.

194 Miller, *Queen's Rebels*, p. 88.

Johnston of Ballykilbeg gave a lecture on 'The Life of Governor Walker', comparing the crisis of that year with that of 1688.[195] Cecil Francis Alexander, better known for her hymn, 'There is Green Hill Far Away', contributed a poem, 'The Siege of Derry', which contained a lesson for later days when 'faction sways the Senate, and faith is overcast'.[196] In 1893 the Rev. Philip Dwyer republished Walker's pamphlets on the siege with a collection of other letters, sermons and speeches; the book included an attack on Home Rule under the heading 'Moral to be Drawn from the Siege of Derry', which called for Protestant unity to resist the growing power of the Roman Catholic Church in the United Kingdom, the United States and Germany.[197]

The great Unionist demonstrations of 1886–1912 also made full use of Orange symbolism and rhetoric. For the most part, 1689 featured merely as one episode in a seventeenth-century sequence, with both 1641 and 1690 provoking more debate, but the contemporary lessons of the siege were not lost on Unionists. Alvin Jackson has noted how Orange leaders like Colonel Edward Saunderson drew parallels with Derry and Enniskillen as they voiced the fears of 'an embattled Ulster, identifiable against the uniform anarchy and political eccentricity of the three south-

195 Aiken McClelland, *William Johnston of Ballykilbeg* (Lurgan, 1990), p. 97. Johnston was a member of the Apprentice Boys organisation and had taken part in confrontations with the authorities in Derry. See also Rev. Wesley Guard, *Chief Incidents of the Siege of Derry. A Short Account for the People, taken from the Narratives of Graham and Mackenzie with Some Extracts Relating to the Battle of the Boyne* (Belfast, and Dublin, 1884); L. Cope Cornford, *'No Surrender!' Being the Story of the Siege of Derry 1688-9* (London, 1911).
196 Cecil Francis Alexander, 'The Siege of Derry', in *Poems*, ed. William Alexander (London, 1896), pp. 149-57.
197 Philip Dwyer, *The Siege of Londonderry in 1689, as Set Forth in the Literary Remains of Colonel the Rev. George Walker* (London and Dublin, 1893), pp. 241-2.
198 Alvin Jackson, *The Ulster Party: Irish Unionists in the House of Commons, 1884-1911* (Oxford, 1989), p. 20.

ern provinces'. As in 1689, Ulster emerged as the last centre of Protestant resistance, a garrison holding Ireland for the crown.[198] On the Relief anniversary in 1886 the *Belfast Newsletter* commented that 'history has been repeating itself. There has been the same bold attempt as was made nearly two hundred years ago to stamp out the civil and religious liberties of the Protestant population of Ireland'; Gladstone was compared to the last of the Stuart kings.[199] Two years later, at a banquet held to mark the bicentenary of the shutting of the gates, the bishop of Derry called for a united Protestant front to meet the threat of Roman Catholic tyranny.[200] The importance of the siege in cementing the bonds of loyalty between Great Britain and Ulster was reiterated; indeed the whole empire was declared to be indebted to the defenders of Derry for 'one of the great achievements of the English race on behalf of liberty'.[201] It was at this point, too, that the name of Lundy acquired its modern currency in Ulster as a term for turncoat. Twenty-five years earlier, according to the editor of the *Londonderry Standard*, the disgraced governor's name was already 'held in execration, as a synonym for traitor', and his effigy was consigned to the flames as 'a warning to nominal Protestants who would presume to trifle with the dearest interests of their fellow-men'.[202] As the Irish electorate polarised along religious lines, however, 'Lundy' acquired a much more specific and pointed meaning as a term of abuse for the small but significant band of Protestant Home Rulers.[203]

As Ulster Unionists found themselves a beleaguered minority in a hostile land, the defence of Derry was rediscovered as the prototype of rebellious loyalism in Ireland. The siege myth underlined the need for social cohesion in the face of danger, and held

199 *Belfast Newsletter*, 13 August 1886.
200 Ibid., 19 December 1888.
201 Ibid., 13 August 1889, 13 August 1912.
202 Finlay, *Siege of Londonderry*, pp. 18-9.
203 *Derry Journal*, 20 Dec. 1895, *Belfast Evening Telegraph*, 1 Aug. 1913, quoted in Doak, 'Rioting and Civil Strife', pp. 213, 251.

out the hope of eventual deliverance. It recalled Ulster's sacrifices for the crown and her pivotal role in the construction of Britain's venerated constitution. More importantly, it supplied a blueprint for action, legitimising Protestant defiance of the authorities in times of danger. Perhaps the most famous invocation of the siege occurred at the massive Balmoral rally of Easter 1912, when Conservative Party leader Andrew Bonar Law demonstrated its usefulness as a paradigm for political relationships in Anglo-Irish history:

> Once again you hold the pass—the pass for the Empire. You are a besieged city. The timid have left you; your Lundys have betrayed you; but you have closed your gates. The government have erected by their Parliament Act a boom against you to shut you off from the help of the British people. You will burst that boom. That help will come ...[204]

In the end, of course, the Ulster Unionists helped themselves, in the notorious Larne gun-running episode of April 1914. With scrupulous regard for historical precedent, the steamboat which delivered 216 tons of arms for the Ulster Volunteer Force was known by the cover name 'Mountjoy II'.[205]

The siege mentality of the Home Rule period became institutionalised in the six-county state of Northern Ireland which emerged from the Anglo-Irish settlement of 1921. The image of the Maiden City was naturally employed to drive home the inviolability of the new frontier. As one Orange spokesman later wrote, 'the Border is secure as a bulwark to [the Ulsterman's] religious faith and his political freedom, under the ample folds of the Union Jack, as were the grey old walls of Derry beneath her Crimson Banner nearly three centuries ago'.[206] Siege psychology was to recur whenever the political temperature rose, but under

204 Quoted in A.T.Q. Stewart, *The Ulster Crisis* (London, 1967), p. 55.
205 See Ronald MacNeill, *Ulster's Stand for Union* (London, 1922), p. 214.
206 M.W. Dewar, *Why Orangeism?* [Belfast, 1958], p. 22.

the first three decades of the Stormont government seventeenth-century memories were temporarily overshadowed by the experience of twentieth-century war. After 1916, the Somme replaced the siege as the great symbol of Ulster's willingness to pay the ultimate price for king and country. In the Second World War it was Northern Ireland's strategic position in the North Atlantic which served to underline her position as part of the United Kingdom; the key theme in Unionist propaganda during the later '40s and '50s would be Ulster's role as the British bridgehead.[207] Derry's historical importance as the bulwark of Ulster Protestantism was eclipsed by its vital contribution to the Allied war effort as a naval base, although parallels between the hardships of 1689 and the Blitz spirit of wartime Britain proved irresistible.[208]

Like Ulster itself, 'Londonderry' was less a territorial reality than a state of mind, demanding the suppression of the Catholic population through the careful manipulation of boundaries in both electoral geography and political language. Given its Catholic majority and its geographical situation, there were obvious political and economic arguments for including Derry City within the Irish Free State, but James Craig had fought for the exclusion of the full six counties, emphasising the sentimental importance of such places as Derry and Enniskillen to his people.[209] Electoral representation in the city was consequently rearranged to secure Unionist control over the corporation. Derry, the second city of Northern Ireland, became the symbol of the institutionalised corruption of the Stormont government. It was not coincidental that it should have been an Apprentice

207 See, for example, Government of Northern Ireland, *Ulster: The British Bridgehead* (Belfast, 1943); W. Douglas, 'The Impossibility of Irish Union', *The Bell*, no. 14 (April, 1947), pp. 33–40; Viscount Brookeborough et al., *Why the Border Must Be: The Northern Ireland Case in Brief* (n.pl., 1956), pp. 7, 12, 14; Loughlin, *Ulster Unionism and British National Identity*, ch. 6.

208 Ibid., pp. 124, 137.

209 Clare O'Halloran, *Partition and the Limits of Irish Nationalism: An Ideology under Stress* (Dublin, 1987), p. 18.

Boys parade which triggered the modern phase of troubles in 1969.

During the Stormont years a number of popular histories appeared celebrating the heroic resistance of the Derry Protestants, but these lacked the polemical edge so obvious during the Home Rule crises.[210] Like Cecil Davis Milligan's authoritative *Siege of Londonderry* (1951), sponsored by the corporation as part of the Festival of Britain, they reflect the more confident position of Ulster Unionism in the middle of this century.[211] It became possible to portray Orange marches as part of a quaint, colourful tradition with little relevance to contemporary politics. For the Unionist writer Richard Hayward, Derry was 'a kind of Holy City, a remembrancer, a rallying-place' whose glorious past was recognised even by 'those whose Faith and historical background might beget a different set of emotions'. The burning of Lundy, in his view, was the harmless counterpart of Guy Fawkes night.[212] Hugh Shearman, the unofficial public relations officer of the Stormont government, took the same view, remarking of Derry men that 'whichever foot they dig with, they are the kind of people who have a way of their own in most matters and they clearly think that 'No Surrender' is a sound slogan.'[213]

There is not space here to follow the uses of the siege during the fifty years of the Stormont regime. By way of conclusion, however, it is worth noting that the story of the siege has been retold to reflect the disillusionment experienced by Ulster

210 James Anderson, *The Siege and Relief of Londonderry in 1689* (Belfast, 1926); William R. Young, *Fighters of Derry. Their Deeds and Descendants being a Chronicle of Events in Ireland during the Revolutionary Period, 1688-91* (London, 1932); W.D. Barfoot, *Defenders: An Intimate Account of the Memorable Events Connected with the Siege of Derry, 1688-89* (Carrickfergus, 1948).

211 As part of the Festival of Britain a stained glass window was also erected in the Apprentice Boys Memorial Hall in memory of Captain Micaiah Browning.

212 Hayward, *In Praise of Ulster*, pp. 254, 264.

213 Hugh Shearman, *Ulster* (London, 1949), p. 320.

Unionists during the last twenty-five years. In the 1960s, when the conciliatory gestures made by premier Terence O'Neill towards both the Catholic minority in the north and the Dublin government prompted fears of a sell out, traditional Protestant symbols were appropriated by hardline critics of reform; the accusations of 'Lundyism' levelled at Terence O'Neill's government provide one of the best examples. Casting himself in the role of the thirteen apprentices, Ian Paisley was to build up his power base by marshalling the forces of grassroots loyalism against 'the ruling junta of Lundies [sic] in Stormont'.[214] Here the siege myth is valued not as a reminder of Britain's debt to Ulster, but as a historical justification of Protestant rebellion. If leadership from above is not forthcoming, the foot-soldiers of plebeian loyalism must protect themselves, a line of action which carries the implicit threat of separation from Britain. In *Ulster a Nation*, a call for an independent Northern Irish state published in 1972, the militant Vanguard movement warned that 'Not only shall we not surrender to oblige London Lundies, we shall follow the brave precedent that the Apprentice Boys have given us and take our defence into our own hands and out of theirs.'[215]

The short-circuiting of political progress by the armed struggle during the last 25 years has perhaps obscured the extent to which political relationships in Northern Ireland have altered since the Troubles began. By 1972 the Protestant people had lost their parliament, and the sense of self-determination which went along with it; the machinery of discrimination was being dismantled, and Dublin had been irreversibly drawn into the politics of the north. With the reassertion of loyalist strength in the

---

214 Ed Moloney and Andy Pollak, *Paisley* (Dublin, 1986), p. 134; for more examples see pp. 119, 121 and the photograph on the opposite page, 132, 157. See also Steve Bruce, *God Save Ulster: The Religion and Politics of Paisleyism* (Oxford, 1989), p. 74. O'Neill was of course himself a member of the Apprentice Boys.

215 Vanguard Publications, *Ulster—A Nation* (Belfast, 1972), p. 11.

Ulster Workers' Council strike, the advance of northern nationalism was halted, but there could be no disguising the fact that a decisive shift in the balance of power had taken place. During the same period, the collapse of the traditional heavy industries which had sustained the Protestant workforce, combined with the rise of a new Catholic middle class, has signalled a longer term social and economic retreat: loss of political power was therefore compounded by new levels of unemployment and deprivation. The demographic progress of the Catholic community, now over 40 per cent of the population, has been registered by the closure of Protestant churches and schools, and the capture of local councils by Nationalists, particularly west of the Bann.[216] A recent study of loyalist attitudes suggests that 'the general image that now confronts all Unionists is one of becoming a minority in what was once their land.'[217]

Once more it is the Maiden City which has registered these changes most dramatically. Over the last quarter-century the escalation of sectarian conflict has led to an exodus of Protestants to the predominantly Protestant areas on the east bank of the River Foyle.[218] The old walls of Ulster's sacred citadel have finally fallen to the Catholic enemy, and the city council now has a Nationalist majority. In recent years business and commerce in the city have revived dramatically; the revolutionary socialist Eamonn McCann, a product of the *événements* of the late 1960s, has commented caustically on 'the haciendas of the new Catholic middle class scattered out along the Culmore Road'.[219] Commercial revitalisation in the city centre has been accompanied by a new cultural assertiveness. The Derry-based Field Day

---

216 Steve Bruce, *The Edge of the Union: The Ulster Loyalist Political Vision* (Oxford, 1994), pp. 48-54.

217 Ibid., p. 52. See also Andy Pollak et al., *A Citizens' Inquiry: The Opsahl Report on Northern Ireland* (Dublin, 1993), pp. 38-43.

218 It has been estimated that between 12,500 and 14,500 have moved from the west bank of the river to the Waterside: Lacy, *Siege City*, p. 270.

219 Eamonn McCann, *War and an Irish Town* (2nd edn., London, 1993), p. 54.

Theatre Company, founded in 1980, brought together the poet Seamus Heaney, the critic Seamus Deane, and the playwright Brian Friel, all products of the local Catholic community.

Nationalist self-confidence found expression in the programme of civic events organised for the tercentenary of the Relief in 1989, designed to convey the message that the siege is over. A 'Relief of Derry' project was established to find non-sectarian ways of commemorating the event, and the result was a symphony by Shaun Davey, specially commissioned by Derry City Council. In the same year a slim pamphlet aimed at tourist readership, written by Brian Lacy, a local historian and curator of the Harbour Museum, ended with the plea that 'After three hundred years it is surely time to absorb the Siege of Derry into a common history.'[220] The obvious potential for tourist development has led to the wholesale appropriation of the siege by a booming heritage industry. In addition to the award winning audio-visual displays of the Tower Museum, the new craft village in the city centre contains the Captain Browning Cruelty Free Cosmetics Shop and the Roaring Meg Picture Gallery. This commodification of Derry's troubled past received an enormous boost during the ceasefire, when the number of visitors to the city rose by 98 per cent. But optimism about the city's future does not extend to the Fountain estate, the last Protestant enclave on the cityside of the river. There the sense of internal exile is plain: a wall mural proudly declares 'Londonderry Westbank Loyalists/Still under Siege/No Surrender'.[221] Community leaders from the Waterside explained to the Opsahl Commission of 1992–3 that Protestants no longer shopped on the West Bank: 'It's like crossing the border—crossing that river is like crossing to the

---

220 Brain Lacy, *The Siege of Derry* (Irish Heritage Series: 65, Norwich, 1989), unpaginated, p. 25. For another account with a cross-community approach see George Sweeney, *George Walker: Governor of Londonderry* (Limavady [1989]).

221 Derek Miller, *Still under Siege* (Lurgan, 1989), p. 73, photograph.

South.'[222] Most Protestants boycotted the tercentenary festivities organised by Derry City Council.

For loyalists at least, the struggles of the seventeenth century still retain their immediacy. In *Still under Siege*, published by the Ulster Society in association with the Apprentice Boys to mark the tercentenary, Derek Miller compares the resilience of the Protestant population during the carnage of the troubles with the bravery of the besieged 300 years before. 'Even should the death toll reach the numbers of those days', he predicts, 'the Ulster Protestant will still remain steadfast to his birthright and the biblical faith which he holds dear.'[223] A similar message is conveyed in *Their Cry was 'No Surrender'*, another tercentenary publication written by deputy DUP leader Peter Robinson. 'For three centuries', he writes, 'Londonderry has been the symbol of Protestant resolve and dogged determination to stand against any threat to its inhabitants and their way of life.'[224] But there is also a new note of bitterness in these accounts, most evident when it comes to the compensation claims made by the defenders after 1689. 'The outline of this period', observes Miller, 'is not dissimilar to the treatment being meted out to the Ulster Protestant of today.'[225] Protestant alienation from current British government policy also colours Robinson's book, completed while he was serving a prison sentence in Crumlin Road Jail for defying new Public Order legislation aimed at Orange parades:

> There are those like Major-General Kirke, who, though they possess the power to take action that would relieve

---

222 Pollak, *Opsahl Report*, p. 40; see also Tony Crowe's submission, p. 363.

223 Miller, *Still under Siege*, p. 58.

224 Peter Robinson, *Their Cry was 'No Surrender': An Account of the Siege of Londonderry 1688-89*, with a forward by Ian Paisley (Belfast, 1988), pp. 17-8.

225 Miller, *Still under Siege*, p. 58.

suffering and distress, hesitate, waiting on their own convenience, before engaging the enemy.[226]

While researching the book, Robinson asked the House of Commons Research Department to establish the present day value of the debt still owed to the Derry garrison. The combined figure was found to be around £25 million or, taking interest into account, £40 billion. 'As the debt is yet to be settled', Robinson concluded, 'it is worth noting that the Province's total Government annual expenditure would be but a fraction of the present annual interest from the debt.'[227]

The story of the Siege of Derry has always combined insecurity with triumphalism, the shutting of the gates with the breaking of the boom. Over the last twenty-five years, however, as loyalist fears of abandonment have increased, their efforts to recreate the confident Protestant solidarity of the past have become ever more desperate. The August and December anniversaries now present the only opportunity for loyalists to recreate the holy city of Protestant legend, as thousands of marchers pour into Derry from all over the six counties. The overriding motif of recent Apprentice Boy parades, as the sociologist Desmond Bell has suggested, is martyrdom rather than supremacy.[228] The siege remains the greatest symbol of Ulster intransigence, but its presence in loyalist literature now discloses a sense of isolation in a world where deliverance is constantly deferred and sacrifice goes unrewarded. Its central components—the experience of encirclement, the suppression of doubt, the purging of traitors, the rebellion of the rank and file, the promise of relief—nevertheless ensure its enduring appeal as an allegory of community relations in Northern Ireland.

226 Robinson, *Their Cry was 'No Surrender'*, p. 19.
227 Ibid., p. 209.
228 A copy of his video documentary, 'We'll Fight and No Surrender! Ulster Loyalism and the Protestant Sense of History', can be viewed in the library of Queen's University, Belfast.

VII

Irish historians have been both creators and destroyers of mythology. Until the early decades of this century, much historical writing in Ireland was simply a by-product of political debate, and no area was more fiercely contested than the seventeenth century.[229] With the emergence of a professional school of historians in the 1930s, however, popular Orange and Green versions of the past increasingly came under attack. By establishing new standards of scholarship, archival research and criticism, it was hoped that the dangerous myths of republicanism and loyalism might be replaced by a purer, more objective history which would be acceptable to all cultural traditions. Few scholars today would draw a distinction between history and myth with such confidence. The reappearance of political violence in 1969 has made historians even more aware of the subjective, relative and inconclusive nature of their investigations. As the late John Whyte found, it is impossible to teach Northern Irish politics in the same way that one might lecture on, for example, Ming-dynasty ceramics.[230]

If scientific precision is impossible, should we then conclude that academic history, as it has developed in twentieth-century Ireland, is fundamentally flawed? In a controversial article published in 1989, the early-modernist Brendan Bradshaw lamented that the commitment of Irish historians to 'value-free' scholarship has inhibited their understanding of the violent and traumatic aspects of the Irish experience, leaving the modern Irish community cut off from the glorious achievements and profound sufferings of their ancestors. He therefore advocated a return to 'public history', arguing that nations need a positive image of

229 For some examples, see Donald MacCartney, 'The Writing of History in Ireland 1800-30', *IHS*, X (1957), pp. 347-62.
230 John Whyte, *Is Research on the Northern Ireland Problem Worth While?* (Belfast, 1983), p. 4. Brady (ed.), *Interpreting Irish History* collects together the most influential discussions of the aims and methods of Irish historiography.

their collective past to sustain them emotionally and psychologi-
cally.[231] Although Bradshaw was concerned with Gaelic, Catholic
Ireland, he added that Protestant Ulster also requires imaginative
and sympathetic treatment.[232] By adopting such a present-centred
approach, however, we run the risk of reducing historiography to
just another medium for ideological debate. At the present time
professional historians are becoming increasingly sensitive to the
inescapable role of ideology and imagination in the construction
of historical narratives, but most are anxious to maintain a critical distance from ancestral tradition.

The purpose of this book has been to turn attention to the
myth-making process itself. It should be possible to recognise the
strength and durability of ethnic mentalities, while still allowing
for their 'invented' or 'imagined' components. Folk-memories are
not spontaneously generated, after all; they have to be communi-
cated from one generation to the next, and this process demands
the selection, simplification, and suppression of historical evidence. The observation that the Northern Irish remain stuck in a
seventeenth-century rut is familiar but misleading. The drama of
1689 has been played over and over, generation after generation,
but it has yielded different messages at different times. What is
striking about the siege myth is not just its tyrannical hold over
Protestant political consciousness, but the multiple meanings
attached to it.

One recent scholar has argued that the siege myth was an
invention of the late nineteenth century, patented long after the
actual events 'had largely faded from memory'.[233] This view coin-

---

231 Brendan Bradshaw, 'Nationalism and Historical Scholarship in Modern
    Ireland', *IHS*, XXVI (1988-9), pp. 329-51, reprinted in Brady (ed.),
    Interpreting Irish History, pp. 191-216.
232 Among the declared opponents of revisionism we might also include Ian
    Paisley, who has denounced 'the re-writers of history who conceal impor-
    tant facts and distort others in order to erect their jerry-built foundation-
    less ramshackles': see his forward to Robinson, *Their Cry was 'No
    Surrender'*, p. 13.
233 Walker, '1641, 1689, 1690 and All that', p. 58.

cides with current trends in Britain, where many historians see the creation of a mass electorate in the 1880s as the cue for the manufacture of 'invented traditions'.[234] Yet it is important to remember that invented traditions are most easily established when they can build on pre-existing patterns of sentiment and behaviour. In the case considered here there has been a constant process of commemoration, rediscovery and popularisation since 1689. Although a distinct Ulster Protestant identity did not fully develop until Home Rule became a real possibility, the raw materials were already in existence, in the form of historical narratives and folk-tales, poems and songs, customs and rituals. For three hundred years the story of the siege has supplied Ulster Protestants with heroes, martyrs and traitors, relics and pilgrimages. The annual street parades have become woven into the social life of the Protestant community, offering opportunities for sermons and lectures, speech-making and demonstrations, drinking, dancing and fighting. But we must also recognise that the functions of this myth have been much more varied than received notions of siege mentality would suggest.

In the eighteenth century the siege could be interpreted providentially, as a sign of God's favour in the wars of religion that followed the Reformation in Europe, but it also provided access to the central English myth of the ancient constitution, allowing first Protestant Dissenters, and later Irish Patriots of all persuasions, to claim their full share of the rights and privileges guaranteed by the Glorious Revolution of 1688. After the Act of Union the siege stood as a constant reminder of the contractual relationship between the Ulster Protestant community and the British state which lies at the heart of loyalist ideology. At the same time, it could be used to sanction resistance to a British government which had abandoned its traditional role as the protector of the Protestant population. Since the 1960s, references to

---

234 See Eric Hobsbawm's introduction to Hobsbawm and Ranger (eds.), *Invention of Tradition*.

1689 have been tinctured with alienation as Protestant culture has turned in upon itself. The self-confidence of Williamite rhetoric has been tempered by a Jacobite note of nostalgia for a lost world.

It is common to deplore the stubbornness with which Ulster Unionism remains mired in a siege mentality; the 'besieging mentality' of Irish nationalism, by way of contrast, has rarely been the subject of academic or journalistic comment.[235] The perpetuation of the siege myth, after all, depends on the plausibility of the narrative as a representation of contemporary circumstances. There has been a tendency to denigrate the cultural identity of Ulster Protestants by classifying it as a garrison mentality rather than a genuine form of nationalism. It is a short leap from this diagnosis to the conclusion that, once the British life-support system is switched off, objections to a united Ireland will melt away. Such an approach misunderstands the reflexes of the siege psychology. The weakening of the union has not produced a reorientation of loyalist attitudes, but rather the shrill, sometimes violent, reply of 'ourselves alone'.

The dominant myth of Ulster Protestantism, with its injunctions to close the gates and man the walls, is often seen as emblematic of a closed ideological system, incapable of responding to a changing world. It is easy to be pessimistic about the prospects of Protestant culture renewing itself. Nevertheless, the ceasefires created new opportunities for meaningful political dialogue in Northern Ireland, and a permanent cessation of political violence may yet enable more flexible definitions of Unionism to

235 The imagery of the siege has featured in Nationalist as well as Unionist rhetoric. Following Justin McCarthy's by-election victory in 1886, the Nationalist paper *United Ireland* boasted that 'The nation holds the inviolate city and means to keep it for all time' [Jonathan Bardon, *A History of Ulster* (Belfast, 1992), p. 403], while the *Derry Journal* welcomed the Nationalist victory at the corporation elections of 1920 with the headline, ' "No Surrender" Citadel Conquered After Centuries of Oppression. Overthrow of Ascendancy' [Lacy, *Siege City*, p. 226].

be found. At such a juncture it is worth recalling the full variety of languages in which the siege has been represented, including the doctrine of the ancient constitution, the rights of man, and Victorian Liberalism, as well as the more familiar rhetoric of embattled Unionism. Loyalist institutions and rituals have been used to express divergences between Protestants of different denominational, ethnic or social groups, as well as to suppress them.[236] This book has emphasised the deep-laid foundations of siege mentality in Northern Ireland, but it has also sought to recover the alternative readings, favoured by Patriots, Presbyterian radicals and Liberal Unionists, of the mythology surrounding 1689.

236 This point is brought out in Henry Patterson's *Class Conflict and Sectarianism: The Protestant Working Class and the Belfast Labour Movement 1868-1920* (Belfast, 1980).

Select Bibliography

MANUSCRIPT SOURCES

British Library
Wake Correspondence (Add. MSS. 6117), originals in Christ Church College, Oxford.

National Archives of Ireland
Rebellion Papers.
State of the Country Papers.

Public Record Office of Northern Ireland
William Campbell to William Bruce, 29 September 1800 (CR4/1/A3).
Corporation of Londonderry Minute Book, 1742–53 (LA 79/2A/6).
James Caldwell, 'Particulars of a North County Irish Family' (T3541/5/3).
Hill Papers (D642/22).

Robinson Library, Armagh
Apprentice Boys of Derry Memorabilia (CX XXXII:Box).

NEWSPAPERS

Belfast Newsletter   *Londonderry Journal*

PARLIAMENTARY PAPERS

First Report of the Commissioners Appointed to Inquire into Municipal Corporations in Ireland (23), H.C., 1835, XXVII.
Report of a Commission Appointed to Inquire into Certain Disturbances which Took Place in the City of Londonderry, on the 1st November, 1883, H.C., 1884, XXXVIII.

Report of the Commissioners of Inquiry, 1869, into the Riots and Disturbances in the City of Londonderry, H.C., 1870, XXXII.

OTHER PRINTED WORKS

(i) *Seventeenth Century*

An Apology for the Failures Charg'd on the Reverend Mr George Walker's Printed Account of the Late Siege of Derry, in a Letter to the Undertaker of a More Accurate Narrative of that Siege (n.pl., 1689).

[Joseph Bennet] *A True and Impartial Account of the Most Material Passages in Ireland since December 1688. With a particular Relation of the Forces of Londonderry: Being Taken from the Notes of a Gentleman who was Eye-witness to Most of the Actions Mention'd Therein, during his Residing there* (London, 1689).

Joseph Boyse, *A Vindication of the Reverend Mr Alexander Osborn, in Reference to the Affairs of the North of Ireland: in which Some Mistakes Concerning Him (in the Printed Account of the Siege of Derry; the Observations on it, and Mr Walker's Vindication of it) are Rectified. And a Brief Relation of those Affairs is Given so far as Mr Osborn, and Other N.C. Ministers in the North, were Concerned in 'Em* (London, 1690).

William King, *The State of the Protestants of Ireland under the Late King James's Government; in which their Carriage towards him is Justified, and the Absolute Necessity of their Endeavouring to Be Freed from his Government, and of Submitting to their Present Majesties is Demonstrated* (London, 1691).

John MacKenzie, *A Narrative of the Siege of Londonderry: Or the Late Memorable Transactions of that City. Faithfully Represented, to Rectifie the Mistakes, and Supply the Omissions of Mr Walker's Account* (London, 1690).

— *Dr Walker's Invisible Champion Foyl'd: or, an Appendix to the Late Narrative of the Siege of Derry: wherein All the Arguments Offered in a Late Pamphlet to Prove it a False Libel, are Examin'd and Refuted* (London, 1690).

N.N., *Some Remarks on Mr Bois [sic] Book in Defence of Osborn. And upon Some Passages in Mr Williams['] Sermon on the 23d of October Last. Sent in a Letter to Satisfie his Friend, a Dissenter in the Country* (London, 1689).

Reflections on a Paper, Pretending to be an Apology for the Failures Charged on Mr Walker's Account of the Siege of London-Derry (London, 1689).

'Tracts Relating to Scotland and Ireland' (British Library, 816 m.17).

[John Vesey?] *Mr John MacKenzyes [sic] Narrative of the Siege of London-Derry a False Libel: in Defence of Dr George Walker. Written by his Friend in his Absence* (London, 1690).

George Walker, *A Sermon being an Incouragement for Protestants, of Happy Prospect of Glorious Success: With Exhortations to be Valiant against our Enemies, in Opposing the Bloody Principles of Papists, and Errors of Popery, &c. Occasionally on the Protestants['] Victory over the French and Irish Papists before London-Derry, in Raising that Desperate Siege* (printed London, reprinted Edinburgh, 1689).

— *A True Account of the Siege of London-Derry* (London, 1689).

— *A Vindication of the True Account of the Siege of Derry in Ireland* (London, 1689).

(ii) *Eighteenth Century*

John Abernethy, *Reasons for the Repeal of the Sacramental Test* (Dublin, 1733).

George Alley, *The Siege of Derry. A Poem* (Dublin, 1792).

An Account of the Procession at Londonderry, August 1st. 1716 (Dublin, n.d.), National Library of Ireland, LO folder 9/15.

Thomas Ash, *A Circumstantial Account of the Siege of Londonderry from a M.S. Written on the Spot and at the Time* (Londonderry, 1792).

Samuel Barber, *Remarks on a Pamphlet, Entitled The Present State of the Church of Ireland, by Richard, Lord Bishop of Cloyne* (Dublin, 1787).

James Blair, *Divine Providence, the Security of the Crown and Subject: Two Sermons Preach'd in London-Derry December 8. 1714. Being a Day of Thanksgiving, Observ'd by the Presbyterians of Ulster for the Peaceable and Happy Accession of his Most Excellent Majesty King George to the Throne of these Kingdoms* (Belfast, 1715).

William Campbell, *A Vindication of the Principles and Character of the Presbyterians of Ireland. Addressed to the Bishop of Cloyne, in Answer to his Book, Entitled The Present State of the Church of Ireland* (Belfast, 1788).

George Douglas (ed.), *Derriana – A Collection of Papers relative to the Siege of Derry, and Illustrative of the Revolution of 1688* (Londonderry, 1794).

James Glass, *Libertas. A Poem* (Belfast, 1789).

William Hamill, *A View of the Danger and Folly of Being Publick-Spirited, and Sincerely Loving One's Country* (London 1721).

William Henry, *The Beauty, Deliverances, and Security of the British*

Constitution, set forth in a Sermon, Preached in the Cathedral Church of London-Derry, on the First Day of August, 1746 (Dublin, 1746).

John Kearney, *A Sermon Preached at the Church of St. Warburgh's, Dublin, on Sunday the First Day of March, 1746-7. For the Benefit of the Poor Remains and Descendants of the Protestants who Defended Enniskilling and Derry in the Year 1689* (Dublin, 1747).

James Kirkpatrick, *An Historical Essay upon the Loyalty of Presbyterians* (n.pl., 1713).

[George Vaughan Sampson] *Remarks on the Present State of the Catholic Question in Ireland. Addressed to the Provost and Fellows of Trinity College. By a Clergyman of the Church of England, Member of the Royal Irish Academy, and Citizen of London-Derry* (Belfast, 1793).

George Walker, *The Power of Protestant Religious Principle in Producing a National Spirit of Defence, Exemplified in a Diary of the Siege of London-Derry...Now Published as a Useful Lesson to the Present Times* (London, 1758).

— *A True Account of the Siege of London-Derry ... To which is Added, Sir John Dalrymple's Account of the Siege of Derry, and the Battle of the Boyne* (Londonderry, 1787).

(iii) *Nineteenth Century*

Cecil Francis Alexander, 'The Siege of Derry', in *Poems*, ed. William Alexander (London, 1896), pp. 149-57.

James Anderson, *The Siege and Relief of Londonderry in 1689* (Belfast, 1926).

John Bryson, *An Address delivered in the Corporation Hall, Londonderry, on Wednesday Evening, May 20, 1868* (Derry and Belfast, 1868).

Alexander Buchanan, *Sermon Delivered before the Orangemen of the City of Derry and the Cumber Claudy District on the Twelfth of July, 1849, at Brackfield Presbyterian Church* (Derry, 1849).

Thomas Colby, *Ordnance Survey of the County Londonderry* (Dublin, 1837).

L. Cope Cornford, *'No Surrender!' Being the Story of the Siege of Derry 1688-9* (London, 1911).

James Crawford, *Alleluia: The Commemoration Sermon, Preached on 12 August, 1864, the 175th Anniversary of the Relief of Londonderry, in the Strand Presbyterian Church* (Londonderry, 1864).

Thomas Croskery, 'Ulster and its People', *Frazer's Magazine*, XIV (1876), pp. 219-29.

— *Irish Presbyterianism: Its History, Character, Influence and Present Disposition* (Dublin, 1884).

Abraham Dawson, 'Biographical Notice of George Walker, Governor of Derry during the Siege in 1688', *Ulster Journal of Archaeology*, 1st ser., II (1854), pp. 129-35, 261-78.

Philip Dwyer, *The Siege of Londonderry in 1689, as Set Forth in the Literary Remains of Colonel the Rev. George Walker* (London and Dublin, 1893).

James Edward Finlay, *The Siege of Londonderry: Compiled from the Best Sources* (2nd edition, Londonderry, 1861).

Joshua Gillespie, *A Narrative of the Most Remarkable Events in the Life of William the Third King of England, and Prince of Orange. Also, a Revised History of the Siege of Londonderry* (Derry, 1823).

Thomas B. Gough, *A Sermon, Preached in the Cathedral of Derry, on Monday, December 18, 1826* (Derry, 1827).

John Graham, *Annals of Ireland, Ecclesiastical, Civil and Military* (London, 1819).

— *Derriana, Consisting of a History of the Siege of Londonderry and Defence of Enniskillen, in 1688 and 1689, with Historical Poetry and Biographical Notes, &c.* (Londonderry, 1823).

— *A History of the Siege of Derry and Defence of Enniskillen in 1688 and 1689* (2nd edn., Dublin, 1829).

— *Memoirs of the Rev. George Walker, D.D. Governour of Derry, and of Colonel David Cairnes of Knockmany, Defenders of the City in 1689* (Newtownlimavady, 1832).

— *A History of Ireland, from the Relief of Londonderry in 1689 to the Surrender of Limerick in 1691* (Dublin, 1839).

— *Ireland Preserved; or the Siege of Londonderry and Battle of Aughrim, with Lyrical Poems and Biographical Notes* (Dublin, 1841).

[James] Gregg, *The Apprentice Boys of Derry, and No Surrender! or, Protestant Heroism Triumphant over Popish Malignity; Being a Succinct and Interesting Account of the Siege of Derry* (London, 1827).

Wesley Guard, *Chief Incidents of the Siege of Derry. A Short Account for the People, taken from the Narratives of Graham and Mackenzie with Some Extracts Relating to the Battle of the Boyne* (Belfast, and Dublin, 1884).

Thomas Hamilton, *History of the Irish Presbyterian Church* (Edinburgh, 1886).

Hugh Hanna, *'A Memorial of the Divine Mercies to our Fathers', Being a Sermon Delivered to the Apprentice Boys, in the Strand Presbyterian*

Church, on 12th August, 1863, the 174th Anniversary of Derry's Deliverance (Derry, 1863).

— *Weighed and Wanting. An Examination by the Rev. Hugh Hanna of a Review by the Rev. Archibald Robinson, of a Lecture on 'The Siege of Derry', by the Rev. Hugh Hanna* (Belfast, 1871).

Richard Hayward, *In Praise of Ulster* (London, 1938).

John Hempton (ed.), *Siege and History of Londonderry* (Londonderry, Dublin, London, 1861).

Historical Manuscripts Commission, *The Manuscripts and Correspondence of James, First Earl of Charlemont*, 2 vols., HMC, 13th report, app. pt. VIII (1894).

W.S Kerr, *Walker of Derry* (Londonderry, 1938).

W.D. Killen (ed.), *MacKenzie's Memorials of the Siege of Derry Including his Narrative and its Vindication* (Belfast and Derry, 1861).

Brian Lacy, *Siege City: The Story of Derry and Londonderry* (Belfast, 1990).

W.T. Latimer, *A History of the Irish Presbyterians* (Belfast, 1893).

Londonderry Working Men's Protestant Defence Association. Report of Inaugural Meeting, &c., Held on Friday, 17th April, 1868 (Derry, 1868).

Alexander James M'Carron, *Refutation of Mr Hayden's Vindication of his Speech: Proving that he has Neither Vindicated his Speech, nor Refuted my Pamphlet* (Derry, 1827).

Thomas Babington Macaulay, *The History of England from the Accession of James II* (5 vols., London, 1849-61).

— *Repeal of the Union with Ireland: A Speech by Lord Macaulay, Delivered in the House of Commons on the 6th of February, 1833* (Dublin, 1886).

William McClure, *Sermon, Preached to the Apprentice Boys of Derry, on the Twelfth of August, 1859, Being the 170th Anniversary of the Relief of the City* [Derry, 1859].

— *A Sermon Preached in the First Presbyterian Church of Londonderry, on Monday, the 12th of August, 1861, Being the 171st [sic] Anniversary of the Relief of that City* (Londonderry, 1861).

Thomas MacKnight, *Ulster As It Is, or Twenty-Eight Years' Experience as an Irish Editor* (2 vols., London, 1896).

[Robert Oswald] *The Immortal Walker and the General Assembly. The Discussion between the Rev. Robert Oswald and the Rev. H.B. Wilson, D.D., Ex-Moderator of the General Assembly* (Newry, 1890).

Edward L. Parker, *The History of Londonderry, Comprising the Towns of Derry and Londonderry, N.H.* (Boston, 1851).

Charlotte Elizabeth Phelan [afterwards Tonna], *Derry, A Tale of the Revolution of 1688* (London, 1833).

Francis J. Porter, *Be In Earnest: A Sermon, Delivered before the Mitchelburne Club, on 12 August, 1863, Anniversary of the Relief of Londonderry. With an Appendix, Historical Epitome, Rules, &c., of the Mitchelburne Club* (Derry, 1863).

James Seaton Reid, *History of the Presbyterian Church in Ireland*, ed. William D. Killen (2nd edn., 3 vols., Belfast, 1867).

Robert Simpson, *The Annals of Derry, Showing the Rise and Progress of the Town from the Earliest Accounts on Record to the Plantation under King James I - 1613. And thence of the City of Londonderry to the Present Time* (Derry, 1847).

[Robert Stewart, Viscount Castlereagh] *Memoirs and Correspondence of Viscount Castlereagh*, ed. Charles Vane, 3rd Marquis of Londonderry (12 vols., London, 1848-54).

Verax, *The Derry Celebrations: Being a Series of Letters, Written for the Londonderry Sentinel in Reply to Some Editorials Published in the Londonderry Standard* (Derry, 1871).

Thomas Witherow, *Derry and Enniskillen in the Year 1689: The Story of Some Famous Battlefields in Ulster* (Belfast, 1873).

— (ed.), *Historical and Literary Memorials of Presbyterianism in Ireland* (2 vols., Belfast, 1879-80).

— (ed.), *Two Diaries of Derry in 1689* (Londonderry, 1888).

Thomas Young, *The Siege of Derry. A Prize Poem in Four Cantos and Occasional Pieces* (Dublin and London, 1868).

(iv) *Twentieth Century*

J.R.R. Adams, *The Printed Word and the Common Man: Popular Culture in Ulster 1700-1900* (Belfast, 1987).

Douglas Armstrong, *The Life and Work of the Rev. Prof. Thomas Witherow* (Belfast, 1985).

Jonathan Bardon, *A History of Ulster* (Belfast, 1992).

W.D. Barfoot, *Defenders: An Intimate Account of the Memorable Events Connected with the Siege of Derry, 1688-89* (Carrickfergus, 1948).

T.C. Barnard, 'The Uses of the 23 October 1641 and Irish Protestant Celebrations', *EHR*, CVI (1991), pp. 889-920

— '1641: A Bibliographical Essay', in B. MacCuarta (ed.), *Ulster 1641: Aspects of the Irish Rising* (Belfast, 1993), pp. 173-86.

Thomas Bartlett, *The Fall and Rise of the Irish Nation: The Catholic Question 1690-1830* (Dublin, 1992).

J.C. Beckett, 'William King's Administration of the Diocese of Derry 1691-1703', *IHS*, IV (1944), pp. 164-80.

Desmond Bell, *Acts of Union: Youth Culture and Sectarianism in Northern Ireland* (Basingstoke, 1990).

Ciaran Brady (ed.), *Interpreting Irish History: The Debate on Historical Revisionism 1938-1994* (Dublin, 1994).

Viscount Brookeborough et al., *Why the Border Must Be: The Northern Ireland Case in Brief* (n.pl., 1956).

Steve Bruce, *God Save Ulster: The Religion and Politics of Paisleyism* (Oxford, 1989).

Steve Bruce, *The Edge of the Union: The Ulster Loyalist Political Vision* (Oxford, 1994).

J.W. Burrow, *A Liberal Descent: Victorian Historians and the English Past* (Cambridge, 1981).

John Clive, *Thomas Babington Macaulay: The Shaping of the Historian* (1976).

David Cressy, 'The Fifth of November Remembered', in Roy Porter (ed.), *Myths of the English* (Cambridge, 1993), pp. 68-90.

M.W. Dewar, *Why Orangeism?* [Belfast, 1958].

W. Douglas, 'The Impossibility of Irish Union', *The Bell*, no. 14 (April, 1947), pp. 33-40.

Owen Dudley Edwards, *Macaulay* (London, 1988).

John Dunlop, *A Precarious Belonging: Presbyterians and the Conflict in Ireland* (Belfast, 1995).

Tony Gray, *No Surrender! The Siege of Londonderry 1689* (London, 1975).

Colin Haydon, *Anti-Catholicism in Eighteenth-Century England, c. 1714-80* (Manchester, 1993).

Fred Heatley, 'Community Relations and the Religious Geography 1800-86', in J.C. Beckett *et al.*, *Belfast: The Making of the City 1800-1914* (Belfast, 1983), pp. 129-42

David Hempton and Myrtle Hill, *Evangelical Protestantism in Ulster Society 1740-1890* (London, 1992).

J.R. Hill, 'National Festivals, the State and "Protestant Ascendancy" in Ireland, 1790-1829', *Irish Historical Studies*, XXIV (1984-5), pp. 30-51.

— 'Popery and Protestantism, Civil and Religious Liberty: The Disputed Lessons of Irish History, 1680-1812', *Past and Present*, no. 118 (1988), pp. 96-129;

E.J. Hobsbawm and T. Ranger (eds.), *The Invention of Tradition* (Cambridge, 1983).

Finlay Holmes, *Henry Cooke* (Belfast, 1981).

Alvin Jackson, *The Ulster Party: Irish Unionists in the House of Commons, 1884-1911* (Oxford, 1989).

James Kelly, '"The Glorious and Immortal Memory": Commemoration and Protestant Identity in Ireland 1660-1800', *Proceedings of the Royal Irish Academy*, vol. 94C (1990), pp. 25-52.

John Kenyon, *The History Men: The Historical Profession in England since the Renaissance* (2nd edition, London, 1993).

Brain Lacy, *The Siege of Derry* (Irish Heritage Series: 65, Norwich, 1989).

James Loughlin, *Ulster Unionism and British National Identity since 1885* (London, 1995).

Gordon Lucy (ed.), *Macaulay on Londonderry, Enniskillen and the Boyne* (Tandragee, 1989).

F.S.L. Lyons, *Culture and Anarchy in Ireland 1890-1939* (Oxford, 1979).

Ian McBride, 'Presbyterians in the Penal Era', *Bullán*, vol. I, no. 2 (Autumn, 1994), pp. 73-86.

— 'Ulster and the British Problem', in Richard English and Graham Walker (eds.), *Unionism in Modern Ireland* (Basingstoke, 1996), pp. 1-18.

Eamonn McCann, *War and an Irish Town* (2nd edn., London, 1993).

Donald MacCartney, 'The Writing of History in Ireland 1800-30', *IHS*, X (1957), pp. 347-62.

Aiken McClelland, *William Johnston of Ballykilbeg* (Lurgan, 1990).

Oliver MacDonagh, *States of Mind: A Study of Anglo-Irish Conflict 1780-1980* (London, 1983).

Catriona MacLeod, 'Some Drinking Glasses and a Medal by William Mossop Commemorative of the Siege of Derry, 1689', *Irish Sword*, XIII (1977-79), pp. 152-6.

Ronald MacNeill, *Ulster's Stand for Union* (London, 1922).

Patrick Macrory, *The Siege of Derry* (Oxford, 1988).

D.W. Miller, *Queen's Rebels: Ulster Loyalism in Historical Perspective* (Dublin, 1978).

Derek Miller, *Still under Siege* (Lurgan, 1989).

Kerby A. Miller, *Emigrants and Exiles: Ireland and the Irish Exodus to North America* (New York and Oxford, 1985).

Cecil Davis Milligan, *History of the Siege of Londonderry 1689* (Belfast, 1951).

— *Browning Memorials (With a Short Historical Note on the Rise and Progress of the Apprentice Boys of Derry Clubs* (Londonderry, 1952).

— *Colonel John Mitchelburne, Defender of Londonderry and the Mitchelburne*

Club of Apprentice Boys of Derry: Centenary of the Revival of the Club, 1854-1954 (Londonderry, 1954).

— *The Murray Club Centenary: A Hundred Years of History of the Murray Club of Apprentice Boys of Derry, with the Story of Murray's part in the Defence of Derry in 1689* (Londonderry, 1947)

Ed Moloney and Andy Pollak, *Paisley* (Dublin, 1986).

A.F. Moody, *Memories and Musings of a Moderator* (London, n.d.).

F.F. Moore, *The Truth about Ulster* (London, 1917).

Desmond Murphy, *Derry, Donegal and Modern Ulster 1790-1921* (Culmore, 1981).

Government of Northern Ireland, *Ulster: The British Bridgehead* (Belfast, 1943).

Clare O'Halloran, *Partition and the Limits of Irish Nationalism: An Ideology under Stress* (Dublin, 1987).

Andy Pollak et al., *A Citizens' Inquiry: The Opsahl Report on Northern Ireland* (Dublin, 1993).

Peter Robinson, *Their Cry was 'No Surrender': An Account of the Siege of Londonderry 1688-89* (Belfast, 1988).

Bill Rolston, *Politics and Painting: Murals and Conflict in Northern Ireland* (London, 1991).

John Ross, *The Years of My Pilgrimage* (London, 1924).

Hugh Shearman, *Ulster* (London, 1949).

[R.M. Sibbett], *Orangeism in Ireland and throughout the Empire* (2 vols., London [1939]).

J.G. Simms, 'Remembering 1690', *Studies*, LXIII (1974), pp. 231-242.

Peter Smyth, '"Our Cloud-Cap't Grenadiers": The Volunteers as a Military Force', *Irish Sword*, XIII (1978-9), pp. 185-207.

A.T.Q. Stewart, *The Ulster Crisis* (London, 1967).

— *The Narrow Ground: Aspects of Ulster, 1609-1969* (London, 1977).

George Otto Trevelyan, *The Life and Labours of Lord Macaulay* (enlarged edition, London, 1908).

Vanguard Publications, *Ulster - A Nation* (Belfast, 1972).

B.M. Walker, *Ulster Politics: The Formative Years, 1868-86* (Belfast, 1989).

— '1641, 1689, 1690 and All That: The Unionist Sense of History', *Irish Review*, no. 12 (Spring/Summer 1992), pp. 56-64.

W.J. Wallace, *Browning Club Apprentice Boys of Derry (1861-1961): A Brief History of the Club...on the Occasion of the Centenary of its Revival* (Londonderry, 1961).

John Whyte, *Is Research on the Northern Ireland Problem Worth While?* (Belfast, 1983).

Kathleen Wilson, 'Inventing Revolution: 1688 and Eighteenth-Century Popular Politics', *Journal of British Studies*, 28 (1989), pp. 349–86.

William R. Young, *Fighters of Derry. Their Deeds and Descendants being a Chronicle of Events in Ireland during the Revolutionary Period, 1688-91* (London, 1932).

Thomas Witherow, *The Autobiography of Thomas Witherow 1824-1890*, ed. Graham Mawhinney and Eull Dunlop (Draperstown, 1990).

UNPUBLISHED THESES

James Connor Doak, 'Rioting and Civil Strife in the City of Londonderry during the Nineteenth and early Twentieth Centuries', M.A. thesis, Queen's University of Belfast, 1978.